DEVELOPING THINKING SKILLS

The Way to Success

DEVELOPING THINKING SKILLS

The Way to Success

Prof. E. Balagurusamy

KHANNA PUBLISHING HOUSE
NEW DELHI (INDIA)

Dear Readers,

To prevent the piracy, this book is secured with HIGH SECURITY HOLOGRAM on the front title cover. In case you don't find the hologram on the front cover title, please write us to at contact@khannabooks.com or whatsapp us at +91-99109 09320 and avail special gift voucher for yourself.

Specimen of Hologram on front Cover title:

Moreover, there is a SPECIAL DISCOUNT COUPON for you with EVERY HOLOGRAM.

How to avail this SPECIAL DISCOUNT:

Step 1: Scratch the hologram
Step 2: Under the scratch area, your "coupon code" is available
Step 3: Logon to www.khannabooks.com
Step 4: Use your "coupon code" in the shopping cart and get your copy at a special discount
Step 5: Enjoy your reading!

Thanks,
Khanna Publishing House

Price: ₹ 199.00

Developing Thinking Skills: The Way to Success
by Prof. E. Balagurusamy

ISBN: 978-93-90779-08-6

First Edition: 2021
Reprint: 2022, 2023, 2024, **2025**

To view complete list of books, please scan the QR Code:

KPH

Published by:
Khanna Publishing House
4C/4344, Ansari Road, Daryaganj,
New Delhi -110002 (India)
Visit us at: www.khannabooks.com
Write us at: contact@khannabooks.com

Printed in India.

Preface

> *"What man needs is not philosophy or religion in the academic or formalistic sense of the term, but ability to* **think** *rightly. The malady of the age is not absence of philosophy or even irreligion but wrong* **thinking** *and a vanity which passes for knowledge. Though it is difficult to define right* **thinking***, it cannot be denied that it is the goal of the aspirations of everyone."*

—SWAMI KRISHNANANDA

Twenty first century is all about meeting the challenges of emerging new technologies and their impact on the life of people around the world. The challenges are in terms of creating and delivering new products, solutions, and services. Certain specific skills are essential to apply effectively new technologies and strategies that would satisfy the needs and high expectations of people. Skills that were required in 20th century are however not sufficient to meet the current challenges.

We are in the midst of Fourth Industrial Revolution (4IR) which is disrupting every industry in every country in the world. The 4IR is all about implementing new technologies and new approaches that can actually provide better, faster, and innovative solutions. It is changing the way we work and live. It mandates a number of skills that are related to thinking. They include among others:

- Analytical thinking and innovations
- Complex problem-solving
- Critical thinking and analysis
- Creative thinking and initiative
- Reasoning, problem-solving and ideation

- Judgment and decision making
- Cognitive flexibility

As it is clear, thinking skills are incredibly important to organizations across all industries. In today's constantly changing world, businesses need people who can adapt and apply their thinking to new situations. No matter what kind of job we do, we are expected to apply a range of thinking skills to the work we carry out.

Thinking is a cognitive process that involves gathering and analyzing data and information, making decisions, and creating new ideas and solutions. Thinking process can follow different approaches and styles depending upon the nature of the problems or situation under consideration. In the words of Mr Narendra Modi, Hon'ble Prime Minister of India, 'Education must focus on **how to think** rather than **what to think**'. If we want our youth to succeed in the 21st century world, we need to teach them not only how to think but also how to develop different types of thinking skills.

> *"Without right thinking, we are all less inspired, less innovative, less resourceful, less socially and globally aware, and ultimately less human."*

—NIGEL CARRINGTON

Imagine how much better our life would be if there is a way to ensure that we made the best possible decisions day in and day out. Well, there is a way and that is called **Developing Thinking Skills**. Learning to master the thinking skills can have a profound impact on every aspect of our decision making in personal life as well as workplace.

Thinking makes a man perfect. Discover how.

E. Balagurusamy

प्रो. अनिल डी. सहस्रबुद्धे
अध्यक्ष
Prof. Anil D. Sahasrabudhe
Chairman

सत्यमेव जयते

अखिल भारतीय तकनीकी शिक्षा परिषद्
(भारत सरकार का एक सांविधिक निकाय)
(शिक्षा मंत्रालय, भारत सरकार)
नेल्सन मंडेला मार्ग, वसंत कुंज, नई दिल्ली–110070
दूरभाष : 011–26131498
ई–मेल : chairman@aicte-india.org

ALL INDIA COUNCIL FOR TECHNICAL EDUCATION
(A STATUTORY BODY OF THE GOVT. OF INDIA)
(Ministry of Education, Govt. of India)
Nelson Mandela Marg, Vasant Kunj, New Delhi-110070
Phone : 011-26131498
E-mail : chairman@aicte-india.org

FOREWORD

World is on the brink of Fourth Industrial Revolution (4IR) that will fundamentally alter the way people live, work and do business. As the fusion of technologies that drive the 4IR blur the lines between the physical, digital and biological spheres, industries and businesses will undergo a series of transformations in terms scale, scope and complexity. While the impending changes hold great promises, the patterns of employment created pose major challenges to the job seekers. In view of these developments, international organizations like the World Economic Forum (WEF) and the Organization for Economic Cooperation and Development (OECD) recommends that the 21st Century youth must essentially possess certain cognitive skills in addition to the traditional technical and social skills.

Cognitive skills are a set of thinking strategies that enable the use of knowledge and experience to find optimal solutions to complex problems. It is therefore imperative for educational institutions to train their students how to think more effectively. Students must be able to

- think creatively to generate new ideas,
- think critically to evaluate the ideas,
- think ethically to arrive at the right idea, and
- combine them together to sharpen problem solving skills.

I am happy to note that this book "Developing Thinking Skills" addresses all aspects of thinking in a style that is simple and easy to comprehend. The book discusses in depth many different types of thinking styles, from concepts to applications. I have no doubt that mastering of these thinking skills will certainly show the 'way to success' in our professional and personal life.

Finally, I must congratulate Prof E Balagurusamy for presenting an excellent compendium on a subject, 'which is the need of the hour'.

(Anil D. Sahasrabudhe)

Acknowledgment

This book is really an outcome of Covid-19 lockdown. When lockdown was declared in March 2020, I was wondering how to spend my time indoors. It was Dr Bindu Vijayakumar, CEO, Institute for Career and Skill Development, Cochin who suggested to write a book on Thinking Skills. This work would not have been possible but for her constant persuasion, support and encouragement. She provided not only moral support but also valuable inputs throughout the project. I wish to record my deep sense of gratitude to her.

My sincere and heartfelt thanks are also due to Mrs Geetha Nayar for her creative and valuable suggestions for improving the clarity of the manuscript.

The material in this book has benefited from reading many articles, blogs and reports. I am thankful to the contributors of all of them.

Finally, I must thank Mr Mukul Seth and his team at Khanna Publishing House who played an important role in bringing out the book in the present form in a record time.

E. Balagurusamy

About the Author

Prof E Balagurusamy is currently the Chairman of EBG Foundation, Coimbatore. He served as a Member of High Level Committee on School Education of Tamil Nadu Government and Chairman of Committee for Development of Text Books on Science and Technology in Higher Education. He also served as a Member (Education), Planning Commission of Tamil Nadu Government.

He was earlier a Member of Union Public Service Commission and Chairman of Consortium for Educational Communications, New Delhi and Vice Chancellor of Anna University, Chennai, the largest technical university in India.

A prolific writer, he has authored more than **40 books** on IT and Computers, many of them are being prescribed as texts in Universities and Colleges throughout India. Some of his books have been translated into **Mandarin, Spanish, Korean** and **Russian** languages.

Prof Balagurusamy, an ethical leader, philanthropist and recipient of numerous awards and honours, has established EBG Foundation, a Charitable Trust, to serve the socially and economically deprived sections of the society.

His biography "**Nermaiyin Payanam**" (A Journey of Honesty) was released by **Mrs Nirmala Sitharaman**, Hon'ble Minister of Finance, Government of India in November, 2019.

He holds an ME(Hons) in Electrical Engineering, PhD in Systems Engineering, both from IIT, Roorkee and a Diploma in Education from U.K.

Contents

1 Importance of Thinking Skills

"Education is not the learning of facts, but training of the mind to think."

—Albert Einstein

1.1 INTRODUCTION

Life is like a game of chess. To win we have to make a move. A lot of thinking is required to decide the correct move. We are in the midst of a great digital revolution. Industries call it the Fourth Industrial Revolution (4IR). Everything around us is changing fast. The disruptive technologies such as AI, Machine Learning, Robotics, IoTs, 3D Printing, Block Chain, etc. that are driving 4IR have the potential to disrupt the way we live, work, communicate, gather information, discuss , and make decisions.

Industries are changing. Jobs are changing. Skill sets are changing. Work culture is changing. Change appears to be the only constant in the world today. We are faced with numerous problems and situations that require proper evaluation and solutions. According to an OECD (Organization for Economic Cooperation and Development) Framework of Skills, employees in industries need three overlapping categories of "skills for innovation" as illustrated in Fig.1.1.

1. **Technical Skills** (know what, know how, etc.)
2. **Thinking Skills** (critical thinking, imagination, new ideas, etc.)
3. **Social Skills** (communication, collaboration, leadership, etc)

These three skill sets need to be developed in our youth, particularly the students, in order to meet the emerging challenges of the fast changing world. With an avalanche of new technologies, new ideas, new products, and new ways of working, thinking will become the most needed skill of the future.

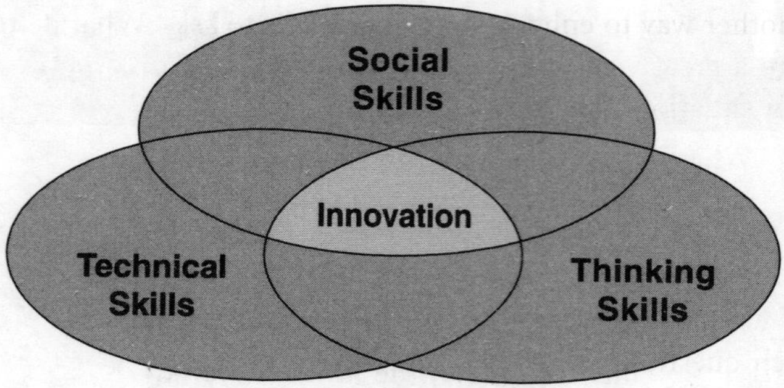

Fig.1.1: Skills for Innovation

> *"Thinking enhances knowledge and that well-developed thinking skill may make good use of limited knowledge or ability."*
>
> —EDWARD DE BONO

1.2 WHAT IS THINKING ?

Thinking is the cognitive activity that happen in our brain. These activities enable us to process information, find solutions to problems, make decisions, and generate new ideas. We use our thinking skills to understand our environment, organize information, make connections and future plans, ask questions, and arrive at certain decisions and conclusions.

When we start applying thinking to understand and analyze various issues and situations, a set of questions would arise in our mind. Common questions may include: Why, Who, What, How, Where and When.

Examples:

- Why does that happen?
- How does that work?
- When will it be over?
- Who is responsible for that?
- What will be the outcome?

and so on.

Answers to such questions would clearly help us understand the problem in the right perspective.

Another way to enhance our thinking is to ask ' What if ' questions. They are a great way to help us think deeply and differently about the things or situations. For example,

- What if it rains today ?
- What if all banks are closed down for a week ?
- What if exams are postponed?
- What if train services are privatized?

Such questions have no right or wrong answers. They do however kindle higher order thinking skills in our brain. It is said that *a thinker is not a person who provides the right answers, but the one who asks the right questions.* We must therefore judge a person by his questions rather than his answers.

> " *Most misunderstandings in the world could be avoided if people would simply take time to ask, ' what else could this mean? '* "

—SHANON L. ALDER

1.3 LEVELS OF THINKING

The National Council for Excellence in Critical Thinking, USA, defines thinking as an intellectually disciplined process of actively and skillfully conceptualizing, applying, analyzing, synthesizing, and evaluating information gathered from observation, experience, reflection, reasoning or communication as a guide to belief and action. The process would help us at proper solutions.

Using Bloom's concept of taxonomy of learning, we may classify the cognitive thinking process into six hierarchical levels as shown in Fig.1.2.

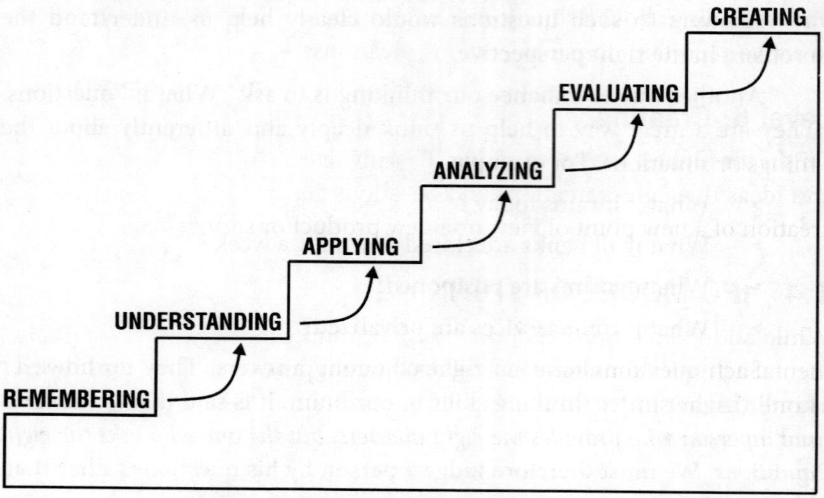

Fig.1.2: Hierarchical Levels of Thinking

Level 1: Remembering

This level of thinking basically involves recalling of facts and information. This level seeks answers for basic questions such as who, what, when and where.

Level 2: Understanding

At the next level of hierarchy, thinking involves grasping of facts and situations and demonstration of understanding them.

Level 3: Applying

At this level, thinking requires application of information and knowledge in new ways by establishing linkages among different facts and sources.

Level 4: Analyzing

This is a higher order thinking which draws connections among ideas. It deals with analyzing the situations and information to identify strong points, week points and their relationships for establishing patterns and connections.

Level 5: Evaluating

This is a critical thinking step. This level requires the use of knowledge and understanding about a situation to further analyze and assess information to arrive at certain decisions with justifications.

Level 6: Creating

This is the highest level of thinking. This involves creation of new concepts and ideas through evaluations and questions generated. This may lead to creation of a new point of view or a new product or service.

1.4 IPO MODEL OF THINKING

While addressing a problem, the human mind gets engaged in multiple mental activities simultaneously. This thought process may be considered as one that is similar to the Input-Process-Output (IPO) model, widely used in systems studies. The IPO model of thinking is illustrated in Fig. 1.3.

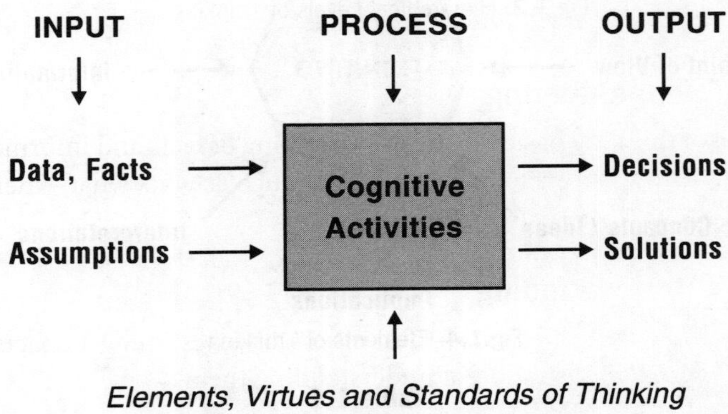

Fig.1.3: IPO Model of Thinking

When we seek solutions to a problem, our brain first looks for **inputs** such as data, facts, assumptions and any other relevant information about the problem. It also takes as input relevant procedures, virtues and standards of thinking that guide the thought process.

Process of thinking may include cognitive activities such as classifying, sorting, comparing, evaluating and drawing conclusions. Factors like personal beliefs, values, ethics, knowledge and skills might play an important role in the entire process of thinking and decision making.

The **output** is simply the final decision. This can manifest itself in an action for implementation.

1.5 ELEMENTS OF THINKING

When we start thinking about a problem or situation, we try to use a number of parts in our reasoning in order to understand it. According to Paul-Elder Framework of Thinking, eight such parts known as *the elements of reasoning or thinking* are identified as illustrated in Fig.1.4. While thinking, we may use these elements to ask the right questions and establish the right connections. These elements reflect how we think about situations. The elements and the probable questions associated are listed in Table 1.1.

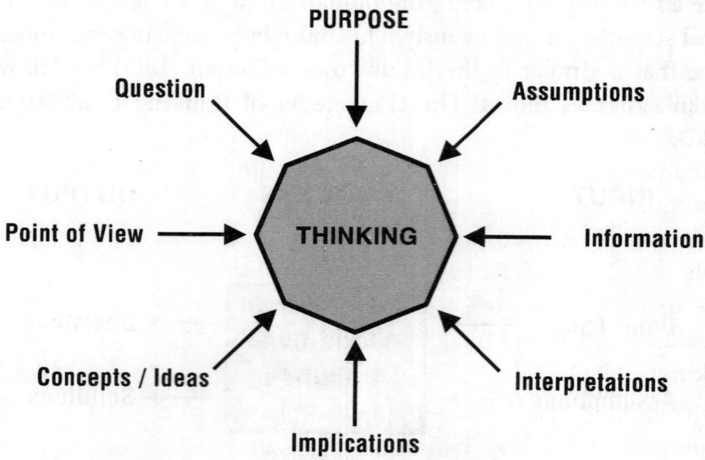

Fig.1.4: Elements of Thinking

Table 1.1

Element	Key Questions
Purpose	What are we trying to understand or achieve ? What is the main purpose?
Question	What is the important question at issue? What are the sub-questions?
Assumptions	Are we taking anything for granted? What are the important assumptions?
Point of View	What is our point of view? Are there other relevant perspectives to be considered?
Information	What kind of information is available? Do we need any further data or evidence?

Concepts/Ideas	What is the key concept/idea involved? Are there any alternative concepts?
Interpretations	What are the conclusions we are coming to? Is there any major assumption we have used?
Implications	What are the consequences that are likely to arise? How to overcome negative consequences, if any?

We must answer all the questions without any biases, prejudices, or assumptions. At this stage, we build a deep understanding of the problem and arrive at a proper solution.

1.6 VIRTUES OF THINKING

Thinkers may be of two types: self-centered thinkers and fair-minded thinkers. When we begin to use the elements of thinking in our mind for analyzing an issue, we may use them either in a selfish way or in a fair-minded way. It is said that the mind is not naturally fair-minded, but selfish. It is therefore important to guide our thinking process so as to enable us to become fair-minded or ethical thinkers. The best thinkers strive to be ethical, even when it means they have to lose something important personally. What are then the guiding principles of ethical thinking?

If we desire to be fair-minded thinkers, then we must adhere to certain moral principles that are known as *'Intellectual Virtue'* during the process of thinking. Some of the intellectual virtues include: integrity, fairness, courage, tenacity, humility, empathy, autonomy, and trust. These are the qualities of mind and character that promote pursuit of truth in thinking. They are briefly explained in Table 1.2.

Table 1.2

Virtue	Meaning
Integrity	We must hold ourselves to the same rigorous standards of thinking and behavior to which we hold others.
Fairness	We must strive to treat all views in an unbiased way without considering any personal selfish interests.
Courage	We must not hesitate to question or challenge popular beliefs when we come across new data or evidence.
Trust	We must always follow the critical thinking process and trust the outcomes.

Tenacity	We must have courage to face any uncertainties and continue our struggle to gain understanding.
Humility	We must always accept our weaknesses and limitations of our knowledge.
Autonomy	We must not yield to any external influences and think independently through proper set of questions.
Empathy	We must consider ideas and perspectives of others in order to genuinely understand their viewpoints.

1.7 STANDARDS OF THINKING

Once we have thought about some problem or situation, how do we know if we are in the right path of thinking? How do we check the quality our reasoning? People usually tend to take biased decisions. So, we need to assess the quality of our thinking.

We must therefore apply certain standards known as 'intellectual standards' to our thinking. A standard is a measure of how good something is. There are nine commonly used intellectual standards: ***Clarity, Accuracy, Precision, Relevance, Depth, Breadth, Logic, Significance, and Fairness.***

Having command over these standards would enable us not only to improve our thinking , but also to arrive at better reasoning. Table 1.3 enumerates these standards along with their meaning.

Table 1.3

Standard	Meaning
Clarity	Thinking must be clear and easy to understand.
Accuracy	All information must be correct and free from any error.
Precision	Information must be exact and specific to the requirement.
Relevance	Information and input data must be relevant to the issue.
Depth	All the complexities of the issue must be explored.
Breadth	All perspectives and relationships must be considered.
Logic	Conclusions must follow from the available evidence.
Significance	Must focus on crucial and important aspects of the issue.
Fairness	Must be impartial and objective, free from any bias.

1.8 CURIOSITY AND THINKING

Curiosity is normally considered as a basic human attribute. Curiosity is an urge to know something new. It makes our mind active instead of passive and keeps us fresh and relevant. It seeks new ideas, information and experiences and explores new possibilities.

Curious people always ask questions and search for the right answers in their mind. When curiosity is triggered, we tend to think more deeply and rationally about the issues under consideration and come up with better creative solutions as illustrated in Fig.1.5.

Fig.1.5: Curiosity and Thinking

Curiosity increases the power of thinking that fuels creative learning and discovery. Curious people never miss an opportunity to ask questions such as Who, What, When, Where and Why (Five Ws) and How. Finding answers to these questions makes their mind stronger and stronger and thinking better and better.

> *"Curiosity is the engine of achievement."*
>
> —KEN ROBINSON

1.9 CREATIVITY AND THINKING

Creativity and thinking are two distinct but closely related cognitive skills. Both require mental effort and energy that are cognitively challenging. Creativity is characterized by the ability to generate new ideas and to perceive the world in new ways, while thinking is associated with judging and evaluating these ideas to produce solutions. In realty, it is not so easy to separate them.

Creativity without critical thinking may look fanciful and ridiculous. In fact, thinking ensures the value of the novel ideas generated by creativity. It is then obviously clear that creativity involves a lot of thinking and vice versa. It is worth to mention here that the curiosity we discussed earlier is the key to creativity. Only curious people can become creative. Curiosity, creativity and thinking are therefore intricately related to one another as illustrated in Fig.1.6.

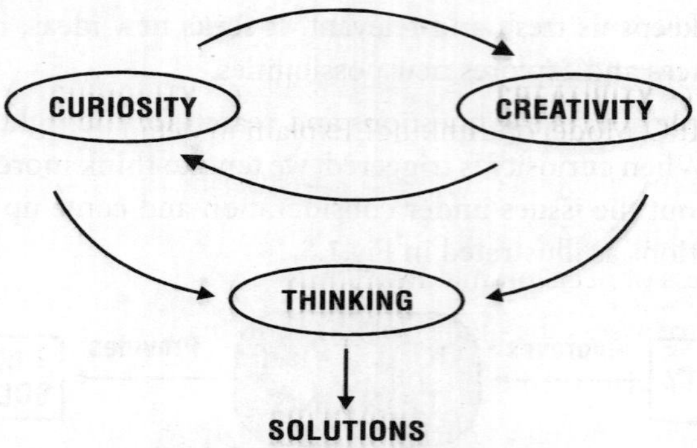

Fig.1.6: Creativity and Thinking

> *"Creativity grows out of two things: curiosity and imagination."*
>
> —BENNY GOODMAN

1.10 REASONING AND THINKING

Reasoning is a process of thinking during which the thinker understands a problem and then evaluates and decides upon a solution. Reasoning plays a significant role in one's adjustment to the environment. It not only determines one's cognitive activities but also influences his behaviour and personality. It is one of the forms of controlled thinking applied towards achieving a solution to a problem. Reasoning requires application of logic. A person who reasons uses various facts concerned with the problem and tries to logically comprehend and find a solution.

How does reasoning differ from thinking? Thinking is a large process while reasoning is a sub category of the thinking process. Logic plays a key role in reasoning process, but it does not have any importance in thinking.

> *"The world as we have created it is a process of our thinking. It cannot be changed without changing our thinking."*
>
> —ALBERT EINSTEIN

1.11 REVIEW QUESTIONS

1. What are the three essential skills needed by our youth today? Why are they important?

2. How would you describe the process of thinking?
3. Describe the different levels of thinking.
4. What is IPO Model of thinking? Explain in detail.
5. What are the 'elements' of thinking? Describe their importance.
6. What are known as 'virtues' of thinking? How do they contribute to the process of decision making?
7. How do we assess the quality of our thinking process?
8. How does curiosity aid thinking?
9. Distinguish between a) curiosity and creativity and b) curiosity and thinking.
10. How does reasoning differ from thinking?

2 Critical Thinking

> *"Critical thinking is thinking about your thinking while you are thinking in order to make your thinking better."*
>
> —RICHARD W. PAUL

2.1 WHAT IS CRITICAL THINKING?

In daily life, we face a number of situations where we use our thinking to evaluate ideas, solve problems, and make decisions. Many a times, our thinking is influenced by biases, prejudices, and inaccurate data. Arriving at the right decision, or finding the correct solution are affected by these extraneous factors. It is therefore essential to improve the quality of our thinking process. We must always look for excellence in our thought. One way to make it happen is, to practice thinking critically all the time.

Critical thinking is basically being critical about thinking. It is the ability to examine and think clearly and rationally about the problems and find unbiased solutions using logical connections between ideas. The aim of critical thinking is try to be 'objective' as far as possible. When we think critically, we consider rigorously all sides of an argument, evaluate their strengths and weaknesses and arrive at a solution without any biases or emotions. We need to engage in reflective and independent thinking. Critical thinking is, in a way, self-disciplined, self-directed, self-monitored, and self-corrective thinking that ensures better understanding of the problem. In short, it is about thinking better.

2.2 WHY IS CRITICAL THINKING IMPORTANT?

The ability to think clearly and rationally is very important wherever we work, and whatever we choose to do. Critical thinking is a domain-general thinking skill. It is not restricted to any particular field, job or industry. Being able to think clearly and logically and solve problems systematically is an important asset for any job. This type of thinking is commonly used by workers and practitioners in different fields of art, science, and engineering in order to take objective decisions.

The Fourth Industrial Revolution, driven by many disruptive technologies, is changing the way industries work and do business. The new revolution places an increasing demand on flexible creative and intellectual skills, complex problem solving skills, and critical judgment and decision making skills. Good critical thinking (CT) promotes all these skills and therefore becomes very important to thrive in the new landscape. Changes will not wait for us. We need to be proactive in up-skilling and re-skilling ourselves so that we can benefit from the 4IR (may be 5IR in near future).

We will benefit in numerous ways by mastering the CT skills.

- Finally, it will be the 'key' to our success in career
- We will have better control over our own thoughts
- It will help overcome our egocentrism
- It will improve our ability to think clearly and rationally
- We will become more objective decision makers
- It will make us better creative thinkers and problem solvers
- It will improve our power of reflection and self-evaluation
- It will strengthen our courage to face real-life problems
- It will make us happier and better citizens
- It will enhance our 'Four Cs' abilities: curiosity, creativity, communication and collaboration.

2.3 GUIDELINES FOR CRITICAL THINKING

Honing up our critical thinking skills may open up a life-time of intellectual curiosity. It may also impose a lot of discipline on us. As mentioned earlier, we tend to be biased and make a lot of assumptions about almost everything. What if some of those assumptions turn out to be wrong or not entirely correct? In order to achieve the desired objective of critical thinking, we must adhere to the guidelines listed in the Table 2.1 before moving to the thinking steps.

Table 2.1

1. Define and outline the problem at hand clearly
2. Gather all necessary information associated with the problem
3. Define, in clear terms, all ideas and points of views of the problem
4. Understand the logical links between them
5. Question the methods used for gathering information
6. Question the sources of information
7. Identify biases, assumptions, discrepancies, and errors, if any
8. Look at the big picture of the problem rather than the parts
9. Find solutions using a consistent and systematic approach
10. Reflect on the justification of our beliefs, values and assumptions.

These guidelines, when used carefully, will free our thinking from biases and ensure that the problem is understood in correct perspective and therefore guarantee the best solution.

2.4 PHASES OF CRITICAL THINKING

The entire thinking process may be divided into four phases, namely:

1. Observe,
2. Understand,
3. Analyze, and
4. Act.

Phase 1: Observe

In this phase, we must observe the entire situation carefully and thoroughly and collect all the necessary information in order to arrive at a clear definition of the problem in hand. We must ensure that we are addressing the problem with correct perspective. We must also identify all biases and assumptions that may affect our end decision. At this point, we may also look at the solutions and consequences of similar problems solved earlier.

Phase 2: Understand

After the observation comes the understanding of the problem. The best way to understand an issue or situation is to ask ourselves pertinent questions about the situation and possible solutions. Asking right questions contributes to our understanding of the situation and thus to reach a clear definition of the problem to address. Questions may take different forms. We may use one of the popular questioning techniques known as 'star bursting' in which six types of questions are generated systematically. This is illustrated in Fig.2.1.

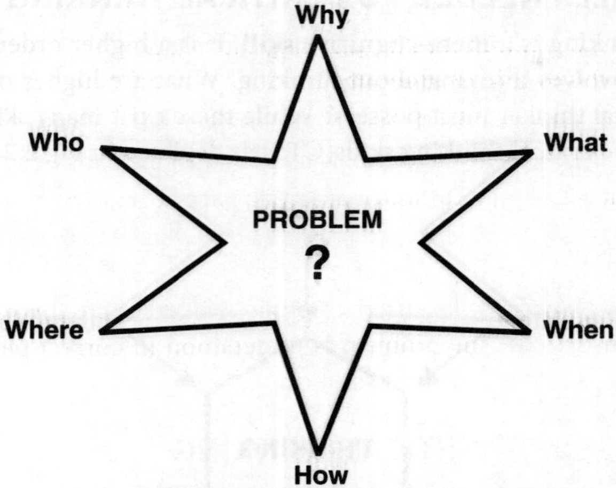

Fig.2.1: Star Bursting Technique

The questions may take the following forms:

- Why do we need this change?
- Who will be affected by this decision?
- What are the different approaches available?
- Where will the proposed change be implemented?
- When will be the correct time to implement the decision?
- How will it affect the people and the system?

Any number of such questions can be generated. It can also be used iteratively with the further layers of questioning about the answers to the initial set of questions. We may also use the elements of thinking (discussed in Chapter 1) to generate possible right questions.

Phase 3: Analyze

The third phase is the solution stage. We must seek answers to all the questions raised without any biases, prejudices, or assumptions to arrive at possible solutions.

Phase 4: Act

This is a critical stage. We must now evaluate all the solution outcomes objectively and rationally, select the best one and implement it successfully.

2.5 SKILLS NEEDED FOR CRITICAL THINKING

Critical thinking is a **meta-cognitive skill.** It is a higher order cognitive skill that involves thinking about thinking. What are higher order skills that a critical thinker must possess? While there exist many skills, we list here six core critical thinking skills(CTS) as depicted in Fig.2.2.

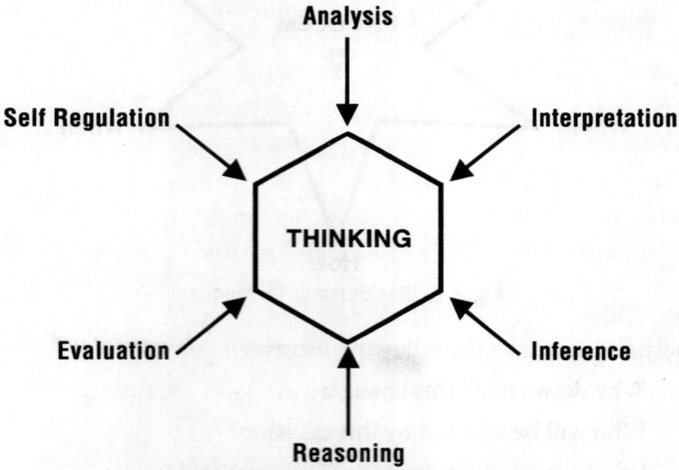

Fig.2.2: Core Skills of Critical Thinking

The core skills and their activity statements are listed in Table 2.2.

Table 2.2

Analysis	• Examine ideas • Identify arguments • Establish links
Interpretation	• Categorize ideas • Identify significances • Clarify meanings
Inference	• Question evidences • Identify alternatives • Draw conclusions

Reasoning	• State results • Justify procedures • Present arguments
Evaluation	• Evaluate information • Assess credibility of claims • Check quality of arguments
Self-regulation	• Check evidences • Self monitor • Self correct

2.6 IMPROVING THINKING SKILLS

Most of us might possess many of these thinking skills to some extent. But there is always scope for improvement of these skills. We need to make a conscious effort ourselves to improve our thinking skills. How?

To master the critical thinking skills, we need to understand three important components which make up our thought process, namely, **Knowledge**(theory), **Skill**(practice), and **Attitude**(mind set).

Knowledge

If we want to think and make correct decisions, we must not only possess sufficient knowledge of the subject or problem under consideration but also be able to apply the basic rules, guidelines and principles of critical thinking. We must also have some knowledge about the people involved, their skills, beliefs and attitudes.

Skill

"Practice makes a man perfect" is a well known proverb. This tells us the importance of continuous practice in any activity we undertake. Knowledge is important but practice is not done, it cannot take us to the goal we want to reach. It is possible to improve our critical thinking skills through regular exercises and practices. Some of the practice activities could be:

- Participate in discussions and debates
- Get actively involved in solving problems at home and workplace
- Seek feedback and advice from experts in your field
- Play games that require critical thinking skills

- Take some training courses
- Engage in independent self-learning

Attitudes

Critical thinking is a hard work requiring courage to begin and persistence to continue till the end. It is therefore not enough to possess only knowledge and skills, one must also possess the right kind of motivation and attitudes. We must therefore have proper attitudes that allow us to think critically. The following attitudes are likely to improve critical thinking skills.

- Being Objective
- Being Curious
- Creative Thinking
- Having Confidence/Courage
- Having Honesty and Integrity
- High Risk Taking
- Perseverance
- Having Compassion and Empathy
- Intellectual Humility and openness
- Active Listening

We can add many more thinking attitudes to this list. We must try consciously to cultivate these habits in order to make us better critical thinkers.

Barriers to Critical Thinking

There are certain barriers that may stand in the way of improving critical thinking skills. We must try to overcome or eliminate them, as far as possible. Some the popular barriers include:

- Lack of relevant data
- Poor listening skills
- Biases
- Prejudices
- Superstition
- Ego-centrism
- Socio-centrism
- Peer pressure

- Narrow mindedness
- Unnecessary assumptions

2.7 CRITICAL THINKING AND FORESIGHT

Foresight is the ability to predict what might happen in future. It basically employs critical thinking approach to arrive at decisions. In the fast changing industrial scenario, it is crucial for organizations to have proper foresight mechanism in place in order to focus attention on the impact of future technological changes and to explore possible alternative strategies to face the emerging challenges.

Critical thinking skills such as the power of questioning, the power of humility and openness, the power of reflection, and the power of life-long learning would certainly be valuable inputs to the development of proper foresight.

A Framework for Foresight

Most organizations started using what is known as "strategic foresight" as a technique to anticipate the future as it relates to their business. The objective of foresight exercise is to explore plausible, alternative futures and to identify the challenges and opportunities that may emerge. Foresight might help us to understand:

- What forces could shape the system?
- How the system could evolve?
- What surprises could arise?
- How to implement desired outcomes?

There are a variety of foresight approaches practiced by different organizations for putting futures thinking into action. One such approach is 4 Ps Framework. The 4 Ps are:

1. Understanding the **Past** experience
2. Analyzing the **Present** situation
3. Exploring the **Plausible** future
4. Envisioning the **Preferred** future

Past Experience

A well known rule for looking at the future is that we must first reflect on our past experience. The process of reflection helps us to develop our understanding more deeply and to make our intuitive knowledge sharable with others. The act of reflection is a great way to increase our confidence and become more proactive in our approach. During the process of reflection, we must seek answers to the following questions:

- What strategies and models were used?
- What were the successes?
- What were the failures?
- What were the causal factors?
- What critical incidents occurred?
- What were the external forces?
- What were the internal constraints?

And so on.

This is largely divergent thinking. If we do not understand our past, we may become ignorant of many of the probabilities and possibilities presented. The process of looking at the past experience with a view to improve our understanding of the situation is known as 'reflective thinking'.

Present Situation

Before looking to the future, we must understand and analyze what we are and where we are. If we are not sufficiently attentive to the present, we may walk by certain aspects that might be critical for our decision making. We might answer the following questions:

- What strategies and models are used?
- What are the strengths in terms technology and people?
- What are the weaknesses?
- What are the internal and external threats?
- What are the opportunities for future growth?
- What is happening in the relevant industry, locally and globally?

And so on.

Detailed answers to these questions and their unbiased analysis would help us understand what is working ("prouds") and what is not ("sorries"), where we are and the constraints under which we operate. We also need to get critical input from everyone with deep experience in the business operations.

Plausible Futures

Having understood the past ("hindsight") and a clear picture about the present ("insight"), we must respect and use them properly, as they are the gateway to successful foresight thinking.

- Identify underlying values, beliefs and assumptions.
- Challenge them and decide which ones to keep and which to abandon.
- Identify events, developments and trends that may have an impact on possible futures.
- Develop possible scenarios for the future that are aligned with the main goals.

Preferred Future

Having identified possible future solutions, we must now choose a future vision that is preferred by all. We may have to use convergent thinking here. The chosen one must be feasible, clear, and more resilient in order to prevent any bad outcomes and achieve good results. It is time to translate future vision into action goals and prepare a detailed plan for realizing those goals.

It is impossible to completely control our future but the application of strategic foresight skills and processes would certainly enable us to better anticipate, prepare for, and manage any "black swans". With conscientious approach to foresight, organizations can better align for success, reduce the influence of chance, and achieve greater heights.

2.8 SIX HATS APPROACH TO CRITICAL THINKING

Critical thinking process can be a complex one and may be even confusing at times. One of the popular and successful methods to organize thinking in such situations is the "Six Thinking Hats" approach. According to Edward de Bono, the architect of the 'Six Hats' model of thinking, the human brain can be challenged in six different ways and each of them can enlighten us with different aspects of a situation or problem.

The Six Thinking Hats

Six Thinking Hats model consists of six mindsets each of which is called a "Thinking Hat". When used for solving a problem, each hat examines from a different angle and brings its own perspectives to the solution space. After putting all ideas together, a best possible solution is chosen.

The six hats representing six different types of thinking are assigned different colours known as 'hat colours' as shown below:

1. **White Hat** – *Facts (Neutral)*
2. **Yellow Hat** – *Benefits (Optimistic)*
3. **Black Hat** – *Cautions (Pessimistic)*
4. **Red Hat** – *Feelings (Intuitive)*
5. **Green Hat** – *Creativity (Creative)*
6. **Blue Hat** – *Process (Managerial)*

Neutral White Hat

White hat focuses on the facts and figures about the problem. We look at the currently available information in an objective and neutral way and also identify any further information needed. Basically, we find answers to the following questions:

- What is the available information?
- What are the facts we have?
- What are the missing information?

Optimistic Yellow Hat

Yellow hat represents optimism and provides a positive outlook about the problem. It helps to identify the value and benefits of a decision. The questions we raise are:

- What are the positive outcomes?
- How can we make them work?
- What are the long-term benefits?

Pessimistic Black hat

In contrast to the yellow hat, the black hat looks at the potentially negative effects of a decision and also tries to find reasons why a suggestion may not work. This cautions us against wrong decisions and wasted resources. Basic questions raised are:

- What are the risks?
- Why a suggestion may not work?
- How can we justify this decision?

Intuitive **Red Hat**

Red hat is associated with feelings and emotions. It tries to understand different emotional feelings such as hate, like and dislike and gut reactions of people about the problem in a non-judgmental way. The relevant questions are:

- How does this suggestion affect the feelings of people?
- What are the reactions of people about the suggestion?
- Are there any internal conflicts?

Creative **Green Hat**

Green hat represents creative thinking. It generates new ideas and creative solutions to problems. It encourages thinking outside the box and is not constrained by rules and traditions. Asks questions such as:

- How can we do this differently?
- How can we improve or modify the suggested solutions?
- Is there any unique solution for the problem?

Managerial **Blue Hat**

Blue hat is concerned about the management of thinking process. It is basically thinking about thinking. It coordinates the activities of other thinking hats and helps in arriving at final conclusions and decisions. It could pose questions like:

- What are the desired outcomes?
- Are the proposed ideas sufficient?
- How do we proceed further to achieve the desired outcomes?
- How do we implement the final outcome?

The Six Thinking Hats approach provides us with a multidimensional tool that can be used to improve the efficiency and effectiveness of our thinking process while solving problems. In addition to problem-solving, we can also use this tool to manage the following tasks:

- For generating new ideas
- For making group discussions more effective
- For improving team decision

2.9 REVIEW QUESTIONS

1. What is critical thinking? How is it different from normal thinking?
2. What are the benefits of critical thinking?
3. How will you ensure that your thinking process will lead to the best solution?
4. Examine critically the four phases of critical thinking?
5. Enlighten some core skills that are essential for critical thinking?
6. How can you improve your critical thinking skills?
7. What are the barriers that could seriously impair the critical thinking process?
8. What is foresight? How does critical thinking help in developing a proper foresight?
9. Describe the 4Ps Framework of foresight.
10. What is 'Six Hats' model of thinking? How does it help achieving a best possible solution?

3 Creativity and Creative Thinking

> *"Imagination is more important than knowledge. While knowledge defines all we currently know and understand, imagination points to all we must yet to discover and create."*

3.1 WHAT IS CREATIVITY?

Creativity is a mental ability to imagine (think of) something new, may be a product, or a service, or a thought, that is useful. It is an ability to generate a new concept that never existed before, or an idea that modifies or changes an existing one. Examples:

- Suggest a new method for solving a problem
- Create a new process for doing something
- Modify an existing process or product to suit the emerging needs
- Introduce a new approach in managing a task
- Change a method of production that would improve quality and or cost

It basically means the ability to think "outside of the box".

We all have creativity and use it in everyday life. But it is true that some are more creative than others. We must consciously and continuously cultivate it to become more creative in our workplace, thus contributing to the efficiency of the organization.

Creativity is an attitude. Creative people will always be ready to accept new ideas, any changes in the system, and be prepared for new ways of working. They have the habit of looking at things differently and doing things differently. They will have passion for innovation and commitment for quality.

Creativity is the driving force for any innovation in an organization. There could be no innovation without creativity. While creativity is the ability to produce new ideas, innovation is the practical application (implementation) of those new ideas.

Our ability to become increasingly creative depends on the regular practice of the following activities:

- **Observation** : Looking critically at the things and happenings around
- **Association** : Drawing connections between ideas
- **Questioning** : Asking challenging questions (why, why not, how, etc.)
- **Networking** : Discussions with people with differing ideas and experiences
- **Experimenting** : Trying to put new ideas to practice in the workplace
- **Sharing** : Exchanging and discussing new ideas with colleagues

If we practice using these skills every day, our brain will become more active and that will certainly enhance our creativity skills.

It is important to remember here that one of the essential prerequisites for creativity is curiosity. While creativity drives innovation, it is the curiosity that drives creativity as illustrated in Fig.3.1.

Fig.3.1: Drivers of Innovation

3.2 WHAT IS CREATIVE THINKING?

Creative thinking is a process of thinking creatively (in a novel way) for solving problems. It is a thought process designed to apply originality in the development and implementation of new ideas or solutions.

Creative thinking is a skill that can be learnt and developed. It will reinforce our existing abilities further to enable us explore things in detail, to make connections, to meet new challenges, and seek solutions that are unique.

Creative thinking thus refers to originality and uniqueness of ideas or solutions that did not previously exist. The outcomes must produce surprises. Thinking is said to be creative only when it is novel, appropriate, reality-oriented, and socially relevant and useful. Skills needed for creative thinking might include abilities such as flexibility, originality, fluency, elaboration, imagination, risk-taking, etc.

Creative thinking normally involves the following basic activities:

- Generating and applying new ideas in specific contexts
- Seeing existing situations in a new way
- Identifying alternative meanings and explanations
- Seeing or making new connections that generate positive outcomes

Creative thinking is expected to enhance the following traits of the thinkers:

- Intellectual flexibility
- Reasonableness
- Inquisitiveness
- Open and fair mindedness
- Willingness to try doing things in new ways
- Readiness to consider alternate ideas and opinions

> *"Creativity is not about being clever but being curious, constantly asking questions."*
>
> — ALBERT EINSTEIN

3.3 PROCESS OF CREATIVE THINKING

The process creative thinking is a unique, new way of looking at the problems around us. This calls for imaginative thinking that produces a novel, useful solution. The entire process of creative thinking may be divided into five phases, namely,

1. Creation
2. Preparation
3. Incubation
4. Illumination
5. Verification

Although we are going to discuss below these phases in sequence, they are not necessarily in a linear fashion. They are iterative in nature and therefore, sometimes we may need to go back and forth between each of them as illustrated in Fig.3.2.

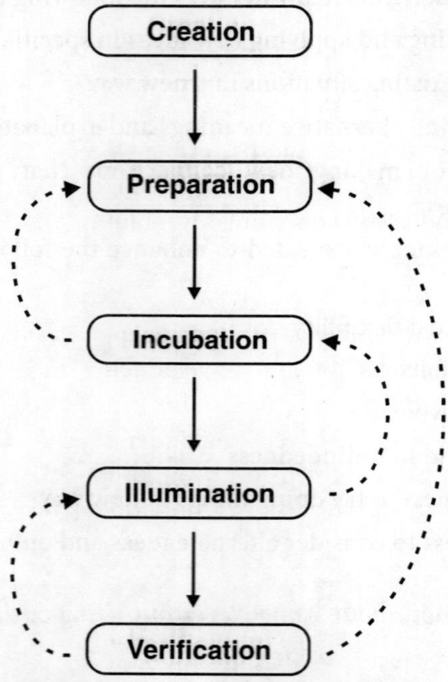

Fig.3.2: Five Phases of Creative Thinking

Creation

This phase refers to the birth of the idea or problem. It is born out of interest or curiosity about solving a specific problem or issue.

Preparation

At this phase, we must define the problem in clear terms and collect all facts, data, information and materials that are essential for finding new solutions. Here, we will begin to think in different directions and look for diverse options. We may use here divergent thinking technique to generate multiple ideas.

This phase is very important because the details gathered here will form the basis for the subsequent phases.

Incubation

Incubation is a silent but critical phase. This phase involves processing of information gathered in the previous one 'mentally'. This means that the information will remain in the back of our mind and our subconscious mind gets involved in creative thinking process such as eliminating unnecessary information, making new connections and seeking new insights.

This is an extremely important phase because it may take a few days, or weeks, or even months. During this period, we stop 'consciously' thinking about the problem. We may be busy with other activities while our subconscious mind is still contemplating solutions to the problem.

Illumination

This is the phase of insight where a solution appears in our mind suddenly. The ideas which have been incubating suddenly take shape in this phase. People call this as the 'Aha' moment. This can occur at any time, may be during walking, or driving, or relaxing under a tree. This happens because the subconscious mind, which has been bubbling with ideas, suddenly brings a solution to the forefront of our mind. This is really a time of excitement.

Verification

This final phase plays a very important role in verifying the solution for its correctness. We must evaluate, test, and verify the solution for its relevance and usefulness. If the solution is not satisfactory, we must go back to other phases for further refinement.

In this phase, we may use convergent thinking technique in selecting the appropriate solution that is right.

3.4 TWO MODES OF IDEA GENERATION

We have seen that generation of creative ideas plays a critical role in reaching a right and useful solution to a problem. There are two approaches, namely, **Divergent Thinking** and **Convergent Thinking**, that can be successfully exploited for generating creative ideas. Divergent thinking is a diffused mode of thinking while convergent thinking is a focused one. Both the approaches can be diligently used in the process of creative thinking and in finding the best solution to a problem.

"The uncreative mind can spot wrong answers, but it needs a very creative mind to spot wrong questions."

—ANTONY JAY

Divergent Thinking

Divergent is typically referred to the process of producing many. Divergent thinking therefore refers to the ability to generate creative ideas by exploring multiple possible solutions in an effort to find out one that is right and useful. The process starts from a common point and moves outward in divergent directions identifying a variety of ideas, possibilities, or perspectives as shown in Fig.3.3. It is a process of expanding ideas.

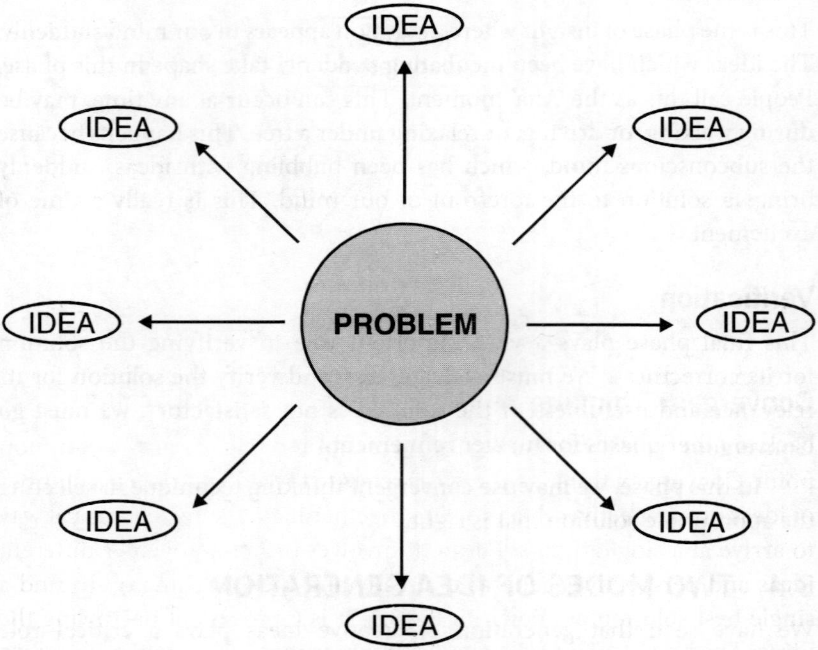

Fig.3.3: Divergent Thinking

Divergent thinking is an ability to think 'out of the box'. This usually requires the following skills:

- Originality and Novelty
- Fluency and Ideation

- Flexibility and Adaptability
- Elaboration and Exploration

Divergent thinking is intuitive and associative and leads to multiple answers as illustrated in Fig.3.4.

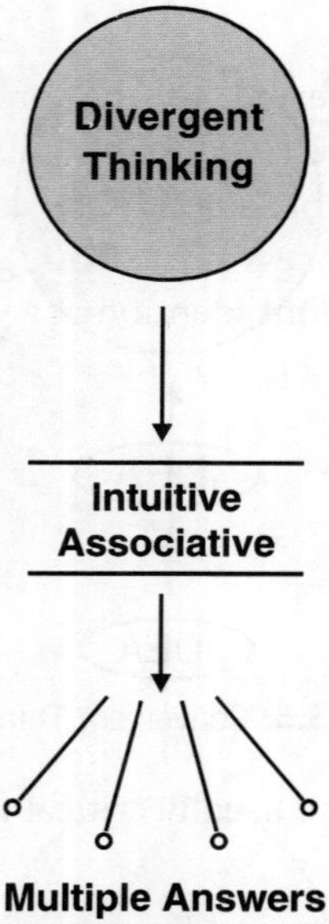

Fig.3.4: Multiple Answers

Convergent Thinking

Convergent typically refers to the process of moving towards a common point. Convergent thinking therefore refers to the ability to bring a number of ideas or perspectives of a problem together in an organized, logical way to arrive at a single right solution. It involves bringing together different ideas and perspectives generated already and then focusing on to find a single best solution as shown in Fig.3.5. It is a process of narrowing the ideas. The best way to find a good solution is to generate lots of solutions and then throw the bad ones away.

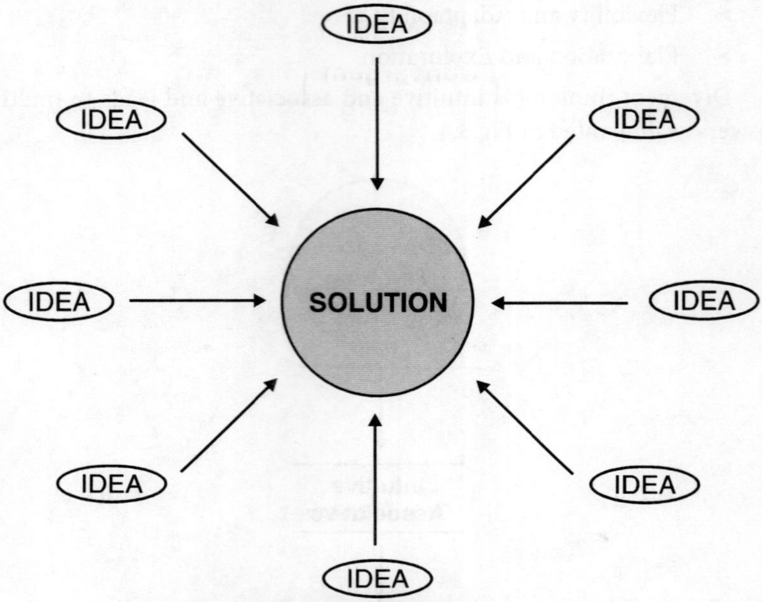

Fig.3.5: Convergent Thinking

Convergent thinkers are usually critical thinkers and are expected to possess the following skills:

- Domain Knowledge and Expertise
- Logic and Reasoning
- Focus and Concentration
- Intelligence and Aptitude

Convergent thinking is analytical and logical and leads to one right answer as in Fig.3.6.

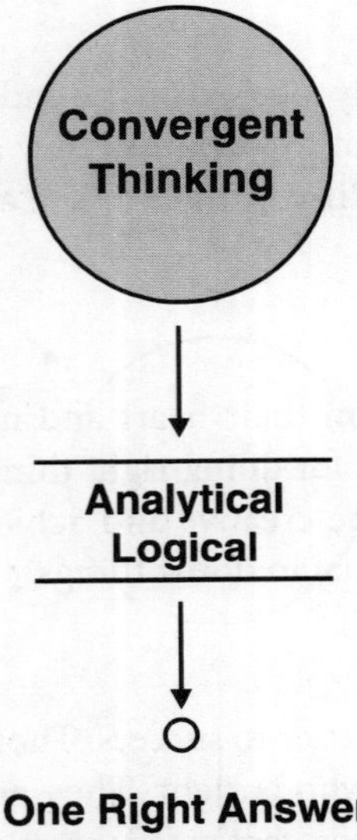

Fig.3.6: Single Right Answer

3.5 ATTRIBUTES OF CREATIVE THINKERS

Creative thinkers possess certain unique qualities that enable them to explore connections, meet new challenges and seek solutions that are original, unusual and useful. They are sometimes called crazy, eccentric and restless people. Listed below are ten qualities that are normally practiced by creative thinkers.

1. Curious Minded

Creative thinkers are basically curious about things around them. They always ask questions like why, why not and how. They prefer to seek out new things and learn new ideas.

2. Good Communicators

Like good questioners, they are also good listeners and communicators. This quality enables them to be good team workers and seek new ideas.

3. Flexible, Open Minded

They are basically open minded people and willing to receive criticisms and new ideas. They have abilities to adapt to changes and to learn from both success and mistakes.

4. Goal Driven

Creative thinkers are clearly focused on the end results. They know exactly what they want and try not to stop until they achieve it. They follow the words of Albert Einstein: 'If you want to live a happy life, tie it to a goal, not people or things.'

5. Not Rule Based

Creative thinkers lead from their heart and not their head. They never hesitate to break any rules for doing right things. They know that if they go by rules, they cannot be creative and achieve what they want. Often they become unconventional in doing things.

6. No Egoism

They know that ego is a barrier to success. They are more concerned with what is right rather than who is right. They never think they are always correct. They are willing to accept any suggestions as well as criticisms.

7. Zero Based Thinking

Creative thinkers tend to practice the concept of zero-based thinking. This means that they do not mind going back to the beginning of the process if they discover something wrong either during or at the end of the process and repeat it with the revised or new ideas.

8. Out-of-box Thinking

Creative thinkers always want to be creators and not mere observers. They think differently, unconventionally, or imaginatively instead of the traditional, usual way in order to generate new ideas or find new ways of doing things. Their thoughts are not limited or controlled by rules or tradition.

9. Risk Taking

Creative thinkers have courage to face challenges. They are not afraid of taking chances and meeting failures. They are full of curiosity and show an interest in the 'trial and error' process of learning and doing.

10. Continuous Learning

Creative thinkers never stop learning. They never think that they know everything and have answers to all questions. They understand that continued cognitive activities have positive effect on brain cells and would help promote mental sharpness and creativity.

3.6 CRITICAL VS CREATIVE THINKING

Critical and creative thinking are two different ways of processing information for solving problems but they can be used in conjunction with one another, if needed.

Critical Thinking

In critical thinking, situations and facts are examined in logical, linear and rational way. The information is critically analyzed, evaluated and interpreted to make informed judgments or decisions. Critical thinking is convergent in nature and analytical in purpose.

When we are thinking critically, we are making choices.

Creative Thinking

In creative thinking, a problem is looked at from various perspectives and lots of thought provoking ideas and possibilities are generated before considering a novel and unique solution. Creative thinking brings a fresh perspective and imaginative thinking to address a problem. It is divergent in nature and generative in purpose.

When we are thinking creatively, we generate new ideas.

Major differences between critical and creative thinking are summed up in Table 3.1.

Table 3.1

Critical Thinking	Creative Thinking
1. Validates existing one	Creates something new
2. Analytical in purpose	Generative in purpose
3. Convergent in nature	Divergent in nature
4. Focuses on probability	Focuses on possibility
5. Follows accepted principles	Disregards accepted principles
6. Process is selective	Process is expansive
7. Uses evidence	Uses intuition
8. Uses judgments	Defers judgment

3.7 IMPORTANCE OF CREATIVE THINKING

Science and technology are advancing at a remarkable pace. Their revolutionary changes are fast transforming our work, our lives and society as a whole. Industry and business houses are deeply engaged in defining the impact of these changes and forecasting the possible challenges ahead.

We need to equip ourselves with the ability to adapt to these emerging changes. It is therefore imperative for us to become more creative and to develop ability to apply creative thinking skills in our work. Creative thinking skills together with problem solving and critical thinking are essential to help us develop our real potential and use it to overcome obstacles and deal with problems in daily life.

We need creative thinking and creative thinkers in all fields of science and engineering, education, research, business and administration including government.

Some important benefits of developing creative thinking are enumerated below:

- Promotes imagination and concentration
- Develops creativity and innovation skills
- Encourages independency
- Increases self-confidence and courage
- Builds intelligence (EG & IQ)
- Improves problem solving and decision making skills
- Ignites scientific discoveries
- Makes people more successful and happy in their work
- Helps cope up with uncertainty and challenges

3.8 DEVELOPING CREATIVE THINKING SKILLS

Knowledge of creativity alone cannot make us creative thinkers. We must practice it regularly. Everyone of us need creative thinking skill now more than ever before. We must get out of the problem popularly known as 'creative block'. This situation occurs when we are not able to crave any creative ideas.

Creative thinking is a skill that can be learnt, developed and improved. We know the famous proverb, " Where there is a will, there is a way ". We must be ready to work out our brain by applying and practicing some of the widely used tools and techniques.

Brainstorming

Brainstorming is the method of generating ideas to find solution to a problem. It is a popular ideation technique usually used by a group under the guidance of a facilitator. The members may use out-of-the-box and lateral thinking approaches to generate ideas in all directions and finally come out with the one that is unique, innovative and tangible. It can also be used by individuals.

Brainstorming encourages thinking differently and exploring many different possible solutions for a problem. It is said that the best way to have a good idea is to have lots of ideas.

Mind Mapping

Mind mapping is a process of generating different ideas and connecting them together in a logical manner using patterns and associations. It usually starts with the problem or issue in the centre, and possible solutions or ideas radiating out like branches.

Mind mapping is a creative and logical way of bringing out our ideas and helps us to organize and understand information faster and better.

Role Playing

Role play is a form of a play in which we define a situation and then two or more people act out roles connected with that situation. Arguments and interactions made during such role plays could identify different insights of solving an issue at hand.

Role play is a powerful, fun, and effective tool for testing ideas and preparing people for unpredictable situations. It allows us to explore realistic situations and improve our creative thinking by interacting with others in a controlled environment.

Networking with People

If we exchange two apples, they will remain just two (or they may even disappear) after some time. But if we exchange two ideas, they may become three or more after some time. This happens when we get connected to creative and inspiring people and have interactions with them on regular basis. Participating in seminars, workshops and conferences is one way of connecting to people and listening to new ideas and perspectives.

Meeting and discussing with new and diverse people will also help us to challenge our ideas and assumptions and thus make us think more creatively.

Asking Questions

Asking challenging questions and seeking answers from within help us stretch our thinking and lead to new and unconventional ideas. Asking right questions at work place would also mean that we are proactive, inquisitive and determined. We must therefore improve our questioning prowess by asking appropriate open-ended and 'what if' questions, as and when necessary. This will certainly boost the creativity of not only the self but of others as well.

Playing Games

Playing games is a powerful way to enhance creative thinking. It is so because games do not insist on the conventional behavioural norms and routines but allows new rules and new realities. There are many different types of games that are available in both the real world and the digital world. We can choose any games of our liking and interest and play regularly.

Accepting Challenges

Courage to challenge certain outcomes, events and situations will make us think beyond the obvious and force us to imagine and come out with new ideas and perspectives.

Challenging certain beliefs and assumptions and asking ourselves 'how could we change them for better?' will help us to think more creatively. Any challenge is bound to bring out our true inner potential.

Trying New Things

We must come out of routines and try to do something new both at home and at office, may be changing an arrangement in a room, or a procedure, or even a system. We may also think of new initiatives that are necessary to face the emerging changes and envisage any challenges in the implementation of these initiatives. Creativity plays an important role in such situations.

We must try to take a path less travelled, whenever possible.

Taking Risks

We must be willing to take risks at times. This will encourage us to think out-of-the-box and look for new ideas and solutions. When we try to avoid risks, we may perhaps leave some unique, novel ideas unturned.

Engaging with Art and Music

There are many activities that could help us to look at things from new perspectives and therefore to make us think creatively. Seeing a movie, listening to some good music, attending cultural activities, going on a picnic with colleagues and friends, and even walking or cycling in parks are some of the activities we must indulge in regularly. Some inspirations may strike us at most unexpected places.

3.9 BARRIERS TO CREATIVE THINKING

In an ever changing world of competition, every one of us needs to be creative and creative thinker in order to cope with uncertainty and changes. Creativity is the key to success. It is the skill of the future. While it is possible for all of us to become creative thinkers, many of us are really not. Why?

Most of us have amazing creative abilities but there are certain obstacles known as "mental blocks" that prevent us from becoming creative thinkers. We must try to identify those barriers and just have to learn how to overcome them. Enumerated below are 15 common ways we suppress our natural creative abilities. If we fail to recognize any of them, they could be the potential blocks holding us back.

1. Aimlessness

The first barrier to creative thinking is the lack of well defined goals and the absence proper plans of action.

When we have clear aim about what we want and how we wish to achieve it, our creative mind will get ignited. We will come out with new ideas and insights thus sharpening our creative thinking skills.

> *"If you want to be happy, set a goal that commands your thoughts, liberates your energy and inspires your hopes."*
>
> —Andrew Carnegie

2. Pessimism

Pessimism kills our creativity. Pessimists seem to focus on negative results which do not promote innovative creative thinking.

We must start looking at things positively and have confidence about the success of what we do. When we are optimistic, our mind starts thinking positively that would greatly enhance our ability to think creatively.

"You must do the thing that you think you cannot do."

—ELEANOR ROOSEVELT

3. Right Answer Syndrome

The tendency to look for a correct answer to every problem limits our creative thinking because real-life problems are ambiguous and often have more than one correct answer. The second or third answer may the best.

Understanding that a problem might have multiple answers would enable us to look at the problem with different perspectives and apply creative and innovative thinking to come out with multiple answers. Flexibility comes hand in hand with creativity.

4. Rule Minded

Strictly following rules and established conventions inhibits creative thinking. Rules are only guidelines and they may not work or be suitable on many situations. We should be ready to break some rules on some occasions in order to generate unconventional out of the box creative solutions.

Creativity is strongly is linked to openness, freedom of thought and going beyond boundaries of what is considered normal.

"Know the rules well, so you can break them effectively."

—DALAI LAMA

5. Logic Minded

Real-life is often illogical to the point of madness. While logic helps us in evaluating the feasibility of a creative idea, it is often the hindrance to truly creative thinking. Albert Einstein said,

> *"Logic will get you from A to B, but imagination will take you everywhere".*

Using more creative decision-making approaches leads to higher rewards but with higher risks. We must strike a balanced approach in order to have a win-win situation in an unpredictable modern world.

6. Seriousness

Taking things too seriously usually causes some kind of mental block for free thinking. Seriousness is largely responsible for why many people find it difficult to perform out of the box thinking when dealing with challenging problems. The more serious we are, the more difficult for us to find creative solutions for the challenges we face. A simple way out is:

> *"To start being creative, stop being serious."*

Creativity springs when there is fun and spontaneity. Fun frees the brain from constraints that block free thinking, makes failures easier to handle, and turns life into a creative and happy one.

7. Routineness

We easily fall into a routine. When we become familiar with the mechanics of doing a task, we tend to repeat the steps over and over again. Many a times, it can be surprisingly difficult to break out of the mold. This is a big obstacle to creativity.

Ideas like "we have always done this way", or "that would never work" should have no place in our thinking. We must come out of this mold and try to take a path less travelled. This can spark up our brain and get our creative ideas flowing.

> *"Great things never come from comfort zones."*

8. Avoiding Ambiguity

Trying to avoid ambiguity may hamper our intellectual curiosity. Ambiguity is the quality of being open to more than one interpretation. It therefore offers us the chance to be innovative in our approach to finding unique solutions.

A creative thinker always embraces ambiguity rather than avoiding it. Someone said rightly so:

> *"Ambiguity is your friend; do not avoid it if you are looking to innovate".*

9. Fear of Failure

Fear of failure is one of the most damaging and imposing roadblocks to creativity. It is not the experience failure that holds us back, it is the prospect of failure that paralyses our thinking and creative process. We might have a great idea but are too afraid to implement it.

What we need to remember is that a failure is a stepping stone to success and failures could ignite creative thinking and provide hope for success. Thomas Alva Edison, a great inventor of all time, said,

> *"I have not failed. I have just found 10,000 ways that won't work."*

There is always a way to do anything better. We must find it out and that is creativity.

10. Fear of Criticism

The fear of criticism or rejection is so powerful that it can, at times, cause very serious consequences on our lives. It can make us withdraw from people and activities and may affect our ability to think creatively and achieve success in our personal and professional work.

We must try to use criticisms to learn and improve our ideas. If we look at criticisms with curiosity and respect, it can become a driving force for creativity. In fact, it can be fascinating, passionate and inspiring. We must remember that: *"Being brave is not the absence of fear. Being brave is having that fear but finding a way."* We must not fear criticisms. The best may come from them. Aristotle, the Greek philosopher, said:

> *"There is only one way to avoid criticism: do nothing, say nothing, and be nothing."*

11. Fear of Risks

Fear of risks or uncertainties is a big enemy to creative thinking. When we try to do something new or unique, or implement new process, it is likely that an error may occur or something bad may happen or the idea may get rejected by some. We need to understand that being wrong is not always bad. One of the key traits of creative people is "risk taking".

Many people fail to achieve their full potential and become mediocre because they are afraid of facing risks. That is, if we are not willing to risk the unusual, we will have to settle for the ordinary.

"Everything comes to him who hustles while he waits."

—THOMAS ALVA EDISON

12. Rigidity

Rigidity is the quality that refers to emotional inflexibility and resistance to change. People with such quality will be unwilling to change or adapt to the changing situations. They tend to apply rigid rules to situations that require variability and flexibility. This is a major obstacle to creative thinking.

They must come out of our own "comfort zone", start looking at things from different perspectives, consider different options and try doing things differently. We must be rigid about our goals, but flexible about our means of achieving them.

"The measure of intelligence is the ability to change."

—ALBERT EINSTEIN

13. Passivity

Passivity is a personality trait that indicates inactive behavior or lack of initiative. It may be the result of inadequate knowledge and skills or not stimulating the mind with new ideas and activities. Mind becomes passive, loses its vitality and blocks creative and proactive thinking.

Passivity is a lifeless monotony, trying to do the same thing almost every day. We must overcome this passiveness if we want be creative and happy. We must act and develop interests in different activities and in doing things differently.

14. Rationalizing

Rationalizing is an act of justifying our behaviors and actions. In most instances, we do it using some logical reasons, even if they are not appropriate. For example, the one who tries to rationalize would say;

- I don't have time.
- I don't have the resources.
- This won't work because ....
- and so on.

Attitude of constantly rationalizing our actions and decisions will certainly inhibit our creative thinking and prevent us from doing something new and innovative.

15. Assuming NOT Creative

Many people think that they are not creative like others. We used to hear people saying, "I am not a genius like him". Such feelings create automatic block in our mind and stop ourselves from trying to think creatively.

We must remember that we are all inherently creative. The extent of creativity really depends on what and how we think about our creative talent. If we tell ourselves we are not creative, it will become true. We must stop that.

Understanding that we are creative somehow and trying to overcome the barriers that inhibit our innate creativity will certainly make us better creative thinkers.

> *"You cannot use up* CREATIVITY.
> *The more you use, the more you have."*

—Maya Angelou

3.10 REVIEW QUESTIONS

1. What is creativity? How could we increase creativity in our everyday life?
2. What is creative thinking? How does it enhance the quality of our work?
3. Describe briefly the five phases of creative thinking.
4. What is divergent thinking? What is its role in creative thinking?
5. What is convergent thinking? How do we use it creative thinking process?
6. Compare and contrast divergent and convergent thinkers.
7. Enlighten important traits of creative thinkers.
8. How does creative thinking differ from critical thinking?
9. Describe three most widely used techniques for generating new ideas.
10. How do asking questions, accepting challenges, and taking risks enhance creativity?
11. Enumerate and describe five most important barriers to creative thinking.
12. Comment on the following statements:
    a. 'If you want be innovative, you must break the rules.'
    b. 'To start being creative, stop being serious.'
    c. 'The measure of intelligence is the ability to change.'

4 Rational Thinking

> *"The great advantage of being human is that we can employ rational thought and resolve to change our circumstances."*
>
> —HYMAN RICKOVER

4.1 RATIONAL AND RATIONALITY

What is Rational?

Rational means 'being in accordance with reason or logic'. When we say that a person is 'rational', we mean that person does things based on certain logic, not based on any impulses or whimsical thinking. The person is said to be endowed with the ability to reason. Such persons always make decisions based on intelligent thinking rather than on emotion.

Humans are not basically rational by definition, but they can think and behave rationally depending on whether they explicitly apply logic or reasoning to their thoughts and actions.

What is Rationality?

Rationality refers to the quality of being reasonable or logical and thus indicates the behavior of a person who is able to make decisions using logical reasoning that lead to sound solutions. Rational persons are often logical, strong-willed, ambitious, intelligent, and self-determined. Subjective thoughts and emotions have no place in their decision making process. Rationality simply means acting in accordance with the facts of realty and reason.

Thinking process exploits mainly two components of the human mind, namely, cognition and emotion. Cognition refers to the mental actions linked with the process analyzing, questioning, evaluating, etc.

Emotion refers to the feelings associated with the situations and outcomes of the actions. Considering these innate qualities of the mind, rationality of a person is bounded by four things:

1. Limitations of information available
2. Cognitive abilities of the mind
3. Power of emotions to override the logic
4. Time available to make a decision

Rationality limited by such constraints is known as 'bounded rationality'. In all situations involving making decisions and deciding choices, the process of 'rational thinking' should be applied in order to arrive at an optimum solution.

4.2 PROCESS OF RATIONAL THINKING

Process of rational thinking for finding a sound solution to a problem is a complex one and may involve a sequence of steps. The number of steps may vary from four to eight depending on how we partition the activities involved. Shown in Fig.4.1 is a six-step model that is commonly used.

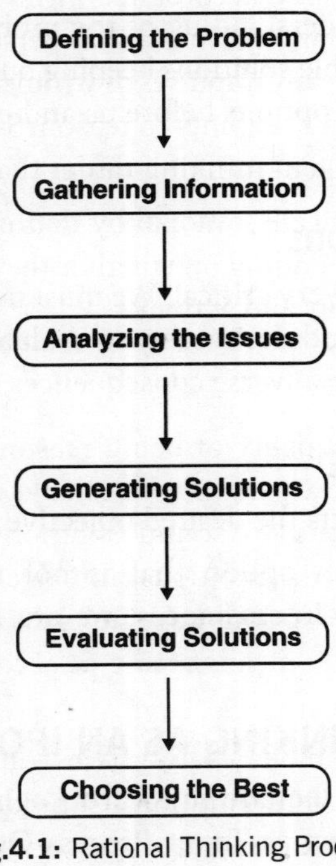

Fig.4.1: Rational Thinking Process

1. Defining the Problem

The first step is to clearly identify or define the problem. It is the most difficult and most important of all the steps. It involves diagnosing the situation correctly so as to focus on the real problem. We must also define the primary objective of the problem.

2. Gathering Information

We must identify and collect all the relevant data, facts, information, opinions and assumptions. We must also try to understand the constraints, if any.

3. Analyzing the Issues

This is an important step to identify and understand the various issues involved in the problem. We must look for patterns and connections among these issues. We may use a set of structured questions to elicit required information.

4. Generating Solutions

Once we have a clear understanding of the problem and the issues, it is time to identify the possible solutions keeping our objectives in mind. We may have many different options before us and probably choose few best among them.

5. Evaluating Solutions

Evaluating the options is very critical. We must use proper criteria such as feasibility, acceptability and desirability to evaluate the options. We must also consider any possible adverse consequences of each option.

6. Choosing the Best

Choose the one which suits the desired objective best.

When we choose an option that is not the 'best' due to some constraints and current circumstances, we are in real sense exhibiting 'bounded rationality'.

4.3 RATIONAL THINKING AS AN IPO MODEL

All the processes, whether they are physical or cognitive, can be represented by a popular model known as 'Input-Process-Output'(IPO) model. The

IPO model is a functional graph that identifies inputs, outputs, and required processing tasks that transform given inputs into desired output. What this model implies is, take something as input, process it and give the result as output.

The sequence of steps discussed in rational thinking process earlier can be conveniently represented as an IPO model as shown in Fig.4.2.

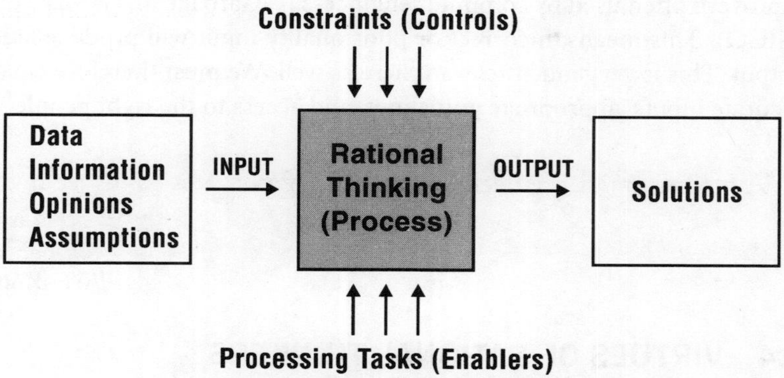

Fig.4.2: IPO Model of Rational Thinking

Input

All facts and figures related to the problem at hand are the inputs. These may include problem objective, data, information, assumptions, opinions and any other details that are warranted. This corresponds to the steps 1 and 2 in the six-step model.

Process

Processing activities include detailed analysis of the issue, generation of possible solutions and evaluation of the solutions generated. This corresponds to the steps 3, 4 and 5 in the six-step model.

Output

Output is the option chosen as the best. This is the final step in the six-step model.

Processing Tasks

Guidelines and rules for analysis as well as generation and evaluation of options are necessary for the mind to perform effective processing.

These processing instructions are known as 'processing tasks' (or enablers). Similarly, constraints known as controls such as time limitation, insufficient information, lack of vision, etc. may seriously affect the quality of thinking process thus leading to inappropriate conclusions.

GIGO

A proverb often used by computer engineers is "Garbage in, Garbage out" (GIGO). This means, incorrect or poor quality input will produce faulty output. This is very much relevant here as well. We must therefore ensure accurate inputs, appropriate guidelines, and access to the right people.

> *"A rational man is guided by logic and reason, not by his feelings and desire."*
>
> —AYN RAND

4.4 VIRTUES OF RATIONAL THINKERS

Rational thinkers are likely to possess certain unique characteristics which we call as virtues. Listed below are fifteen virtues that are known to be commonly exhibited by the so called rational thinkers. If we want to be known as rational thinkers, then we must endeavour to practice some these virtues in daily life regularly.

1. Curiosity

They are always curious. Have strong desire to know or learn something new. Have the habit of asking questions like why and why not.

2. Simplicity

They are simple in living. Never exhibit extravagance or luxury in life. They follow the concept of 'simple living and high thinking'.

3. Humility

They are always humble. They talk less and listen more. Never show their scholarship, power and pride in public.

4. Honesty

They believe in the dictum 'honesty is the best policy' and therefore strive to be honest as for as possible. They do not do anything that is morally and ethically wrong.

5. Perfection

They are perfectionists. Never compromise quality in their work. Anything that is less than perfection is unacceptable to them.

6. Precision

They always look for precision in their work. Never compromise exactness and accuracy for the sack of completing a work.

7. Strong Will Power

They possess strong will power. Have the ability to control any impulses and emotions.

8. Evidence

They scrupulously follow evidences in thinking and reasoning while making choices.

9. Sacrifice

They are ready to relinquish. Never hesitate to sacrifice or give up anything for establishing truth. They know that the tree of success grows on the seeds of sacrifice.

10. Empiricism

They strongly believe that the true knowledge is derived from experiences and therefore experience is essential in the formation of ideas.

11. Reasonableness

They are cool and apply reasons in all judgments. Look for relevant facts and figures that are essential for decision making.

12. Future Oriented

They always think about the future, anticipate future consequences, and plan ahead before acting.

13. Quick Decision Making

They make decisions fast through logical reasoning. Quick decision making is a great skill that every one of us must possess.

14. Plan Oriented

They believe in good planning before acting. Good planning minimizes the cost of operations and eliminates unproductive efforts.

15. Continuous Learning

They strongly support continuous learning which is essential to improve their knowledge, skills and tools necessary to face the emerging challenges in the workplace.

4.5 BREAKING NEGATIVE THOUGHTS BY RATIONALITY

Negative thinking is a thought process where we tend to see the worst in everything. Negative thinking appears to be more prevalent among many of us than positive thinking. Negative thinking happens when we:

- Approach issues reluctantly with fear,
- Criticize ourselves for mistakes and failures,
- Doubt our own knowledge and skills,
- Expect failures in our work,
- Fear the future challenges, and
- Get ourselves detached from work.

Negative thinking can manifest into a pattern that may cause tremendous stress and worry over the time. This might damage our confidence, harm our performance, and paralyzes our mental skills.

Many studies on thought processes of people have categorized negative thoughts into the following four types:

1. Feelings of inadequacy,
2. Worrier that our performance in the job will be poor,
3. Anxiety that some external forces will undermine our efforts, and
4. Worries about the comments and reactions of other people.

It is very important to break such negative thoughts and make efforts to overcome them. One way to achieve this is to challenge them rationally. We must ask ourselves whether the thought is reasonable or not. We give below some possible rational questions we must ask ourselves so as to challenge the negative thoughts listed above.

Feelings of Inadequacy

- Do we have sufficient knowledge and skills to do the job?
- Do we have required experience to carry out the work?
- Do we have proper planning and preparations?

If the answer to all these questions is 'yes', then we are adequately prepared for our work. There is nothing to worry. If we are still worried, then there is something wrong in setting our standards and goals. May be we are setting them at higher levels. Remember here, our goals must always be realistically optimistic and achievable.

Performance Worries

- Do we have the required training for the particular job?
- Do we have all the necessary details, information, and resources?
- Have we identified correct people for the job?
- Have we prepared a proper work schedule with timelines?

If 'yes' for all these questions, then we are in the correct track and need not worry. However, if it is 'no', we must take care of these issues immediately.

Influence of External Forces

- Do we have a proper contingency plan?
- Have we identified all possible risks and plans to face them?
- Have we involved all the people concerned in the process?

If so, we are well prepared to face any potential problems that might arise. We need not worry about any other factors.

Worries about Others Reactions

- Have we made all necessary preparations well?
- Have we put in our best efforts in doing the job?
- Have we considered all aspects without any bias or prejudice?

If 'yes', then we have nothing to worry about others. All fair people will appreciate our efforts. We must rise above any unfair criticisms and ignore them.

The mind is neutral energy. The way we think determines whether the outcome is positive and useful, or negative and useless. We must therefore try our best to pursue positive thinking in order to change our mental attitude.

Although the power of negative thinking is very strong, we can overcome it with some conscious efforts on our part. Few suggestions to overcome negative thinking are listed below:

1. Whenever a negative thought comes to our mind, we must try to replace it with a positive one.
2. If we happen to visualize a failure, we must try to visualize success instead.
3. If we happen to face a failure, then we must consider it as a stepping stone for success. It is failure that gives proper perspective on success.
4. We must resist using the phrase " we cannot " as far as possible. Instead, we must say, " we can ".
5. We must avoid using negative words in our conversations, change them into positive words.
6. We must try to look at everything with a positive attitude.

Negative thinking has a serious impact on every one's life. It may lead to failures, unhappiness, dissatisfaction, worries and fears. We must set ourselves free from negative thoughts by trying to practice the process of rational thinking.

4.6 RATIONAL VS LOGICAL THINKING

We often say that so-and-so is not logical or so-and-so is not rational. Most of the time, these words are used synonymously to mean the same thing. However, they have entirely different meanings. The primary difference is that rational is subject to personal opinion, where as logic is an actual science and does not depend on opinions.

Rational

Rational thinking involves use of reasoning in decision making process.

A rational thinker is not guided by emotions or feelings. For example, a judge is a rational thinker because he always uses reasoning rather than emotions in arriving at his verdict while rendering justice.

A rational person thinks and behaves in an orderly manner. He is guided by his knowledge, past experience and perceptions. We usually call rational thinkers as 'rational people'.

Logical

Logic is a scientific process that follows a clearly defined set of rules. Therefore logical thinkers make use of well-defined rules in step-by-step manner in their decision making process to arrive at a solution. Logical thinkers can also reason deductively. Planners, computer programmers and mathematicians rely more heavily on logical thinking.

A logical person thinks in a disciplined manner. His thoughts are based on the facts and evidence he gathers and not on his guts. Simply, logical thinking means incorporating logic into one's thinking process when trying to find solution to a problem. It sets aside assumptions and biases.

> *"Think rationally, feel humanly, act conscientiously and the world will become a real progressive abode of peace."*
>
> —Abhijit Naskar

4.7 REVIEW QUESTIONS

1. What do you mean by rationality? How is it important for human beings?
2. What is bounded rationality?
3. Describe briefly the process of rational thinking.
4. Explain the components of IPO model of rational thinking.
5. What are the unique characteristics of rational thinkers?
6. What is negative thought? Describe different types of negative thought.
7. What are the consequences of negative thinking? How can we overcome them?
8. How does rational thinking differ from logical thinking?

5 Design Thinking

> *"You can design and create, and build the wonderful place in the world. But it takes people to make the dream a reality."*
>
> —WALT DISNEY

5.1 INTRODUCTION

Today, the world is facing many different kinds of challenges due to rapid developments in science and technology. Consequently, industries and business houses find that the methods and approaches they have been using previously to solve many of their problems are no longer useful and effective in solving the new wave of problems. They are under tremendous pressure to innovate and develop new kind of thinking and new approaches to find better solutions to the current problems they face.

Many of them realized that innovation is the key to progress and success. The ability to conceive new ideas that are effective and useful is critical to maintain or further advance their positions in the world market. That is where the ' Design Thinking ' comes in. This stands as a testimony for the proverb, " Necessity is the mother of invention ". Tim Brown, CEO of IDEO says,

"*Design thinking is a human-centered approach to innovation that draws from designer's toolkit to integrate the needs of people, the possibilities of technology, and the requirements for business success.*"

We all know that design thinking is not a very new idea of this century, but it is the one that got the attention of various sectors across the globe in recent days. It has been credited with remarkable feats, like transforming many sick companies into profit-making ones.

Current scenario is that leading organizations like Apple, IBM, SAP, PepsiCo, Uber, Bank of America, Infosys, GE Healthcare, Marriott,

Starbucks, etc. have started adopting design thinking (DT) as an integral part of their operations. Some of them have even created dedicated DT labs in their organizations.

5.2 WHAT IS DESIGN THINKING?

Design thinking is a unique and innovative approach for providing solutions to the problems. It is an iterative process which favours ongoing experimentation until the right solution is found. It is **unique** because it is user-centric and solution-based. It is **innovative** because it uses a blend of logic and emotion.

Design thinking approaches problem solving from a user perspective and tries to combine three essential components, namely, technical **feasibility**, economic **viability**, and user **desirability** as illustrated in Fig.5.1.

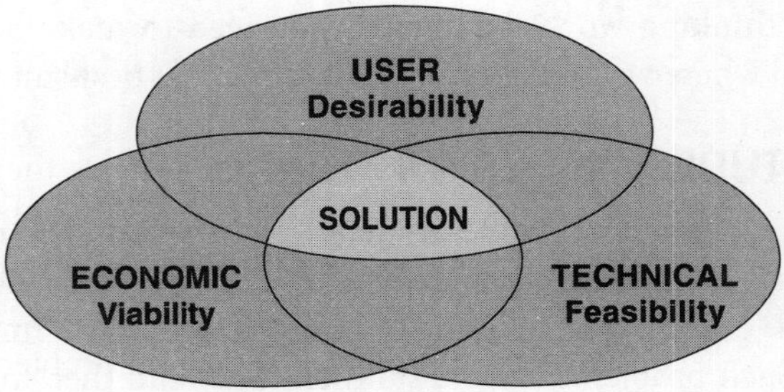

Fig.5.1: Components of Design Thinking

User Desirability

The desired solution must be meaningful and satisfy the requirements and desires of the users.

Economic Viability

The solution must be economically viable so that the organization can afford to implement it. That is, it would be able to create value for the investor.

Technical Feasibility

Technical feasibility means that the solution should be easily implementable with available technology and resources.

Design thinking is well suited to address a variety of problems and wide range of challenges. Following situations are perhaps considered as best for bringing out innovative solutions:

- Quality and cost issues
- Complex employee problems
- Problems affecting diverse groups of people
- Rapidly changing global market challenges
- Coping with the rapid technological changes
- Re-inventing business models and operations
- Complex societal problems
- Medical challenges
- Educational reforms
- Banking and financial issues

Design thinking works best where we need to make human sense of things and where we need to create solutions that best suit user needs.

5.3 FEATURES OF DESIGN THINKING

Today, organizations worldwide are facing a large number of problems that are multi-faceted and complex in nature. The disruptions in human development caused by the industrial revolution have further added challenges. Such problems are multidimensional and therefore require a different outlook to solve them. Design thinking as a strategy may be of great help here. It will not only help them arrive at an optimum solution, but also make them globally competitive. Some of the features of design thinking that made it popular for problem solving are:

- Encourages out-of-the-box thinking
- Promotes collaboration to generate creative ideas
- Provides flexibility to paths
- Helps in optimization of capabilities
- Helps in the analysis of feasibility and viability of solutions
- Discovers the needs of customers
- Improves clients' and end users' quality of service
- Finds simplicity in complexities
- Leverages the diverse ideas of innovation

- Could develop a variety of concepts, products, services, and processes
- Can transform individual insights and vague ideas into reality
- helps in tackling "wicked" problems

We now can sum up design thinking as "*an action-oriented and solution-focused problem solving methodology that primarily leverages the users' needs and the inputs along with the designer's creativity, logic, and systematic reasoning to integrate technological possibilities and business strategy*".

Wicked Problems

A wicked problem is a complex social problem that is difficult or sometimes impossible to solve. Wicked problems that are usually subject to real-world constraints lack clarity and therefore defy a definite solution. However, we can certainly attempt to mitigate any negative effects of these problems by using the principles of design thinking. Typical examples of wicked problems are:

- Poverty,
- Climate change,
- Quality of education,
- Public health,
- Pollution,
- Equality,
- Sustainability etc

Finding solutions to these problems are very difficult due to reasons such as incomplete or contradictory knowledge, the number of opinions involved, the large economic burden, and the interconnected nature of these problems with other problems.

The term 'wicked problem' was first coined by Professors Horst Rittel and Melvin Webber of University of California at Berkeley in 1973 while developing a paper on "Dilemmas in General Theory of Planning". They described ten characteristics that are unique to wicked problems.

1. They lack a definitive formulation.
2. They have no stopping rule as there is no way to understand that a solution is arrived.

3. Their solutions are not true or false, only good or bad.
4. There is no way to test their solutions.
5. Their solutions cannot be obtained through trial and error approach.
6. They do not have specified number possible solutions.
7. All wicked problems are unique in nature.
8. Wicked problems can be considered as the symptom of other problems.
9. A wicked problem can be described in many different ways based on one's perception.
10. Solution providers are fully responsible for the consequences of the solution they generate.

5.4 CRITICAL SUCCESS FACTORS

For every major work, there are some elements that are primarily responsible for its success. Such elements are called 'critical success factors'. For making design thinking process successful in its entirety, we need to focus on four essential aspects, namely,

- Right **Culture,**
- Competent **Team,**
- Conducive **Environment**, and
- Correct **Strategy**

as illustrated in Fig.5.2.

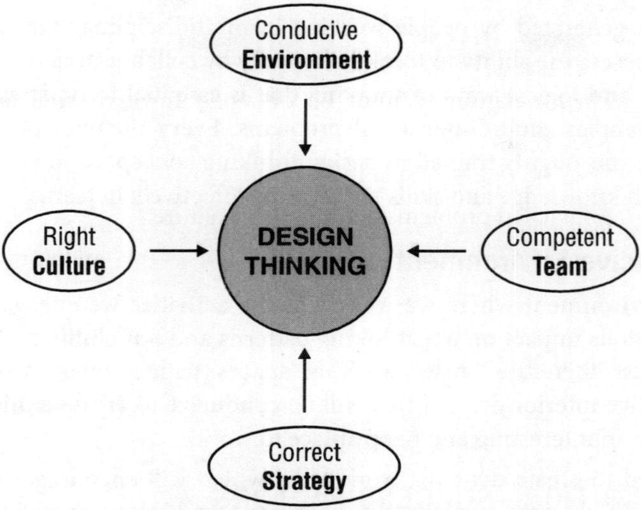

Fig.5.2: Critical Success Factors

Right Culture

One of the amazing things about creative and genius people is the strong connection between their creative and analytical thinking. They are able to blend judiciously creative thinking with their analytical abilities to bring about breakthroughs in their work. We must realize that logic will take us from one point another, but imagination will take us from one point to *everywhere.*

We need to create an open, collaborative, explorative culture in the organization and a creative mindset among the workforce. They should be willing to combine both logic and emotion in order to create new and innovative solutions. With a right culture and a positive mindset of people, organizations can certainly challenge even the most complex and tricky ('wicked') problems.

It is also important that in order to implement DT it is necessary to foster a culture that promotes empathy towards users and co-workers. People working on DT projects should be willing to work under circumstances of uncertainty and ambiguity.

Competent Team

Competencies of people working in the team are critical resources for their innovation capability. Innovative solutions to complex problems are best generated by people working in multidisciplinary teams. They must possess the ability to think holistically by collaborating between the creative and logical ways of thinking that is essential to understand and solve complex multidimensional problems. Every member of the team must be thoroughly trained in design thinking concepts and also possess in-depth knowledge and skills for working effectively in teams.

Conducive Environment

The environment where we work and the activities we engage in have tremendous impact on our thinking patterns and our ability to innovate. We must therefore create working spaces with proper layouts and innovative interior designs that will be conducive to creative thinking. It must be an interesting and happy place to work.

We need to create dynamic work areas which will encourage people to appreciate changes, explore new initiatives and new ways of thinking, and work together collaboratively. Many leading companies spend a lot of time and money in creating playful workspaces with an aim of helping employees not only to feel safe but also to come out with innovative ideas in a playful manner.

Correct Strategy

For any project to succeed, it is absolutely essential to have the full support of the management. The management must therefore have a clear strategy for implementing the DT project. The DT team requires support in terms of manpower, funds, tools, and physical spaces as well as cooperation of other employees.

Since design thinking is likely to challenge the organizational power structure and culture, the management must firmly communicate their support and encouragement to their employees for implementing DT related activities.

5.5 PRINCIPLES OF DESIGN THINKING

As we stated earlier, design thinking is a highly user-centric and iterative process aimed at arriving at a tangible solution. There are always certain basic principles that govern every activity we undertake. Design thinking is no exception. According to the Institute of Design at Stanford University, USA, there are four principles or rules that guide people working in design thinking as shown in Fig.5.3.

1. Human Rule
2. Ambiguity Rule
3. Re-design Rule
4. Tangibility Rule

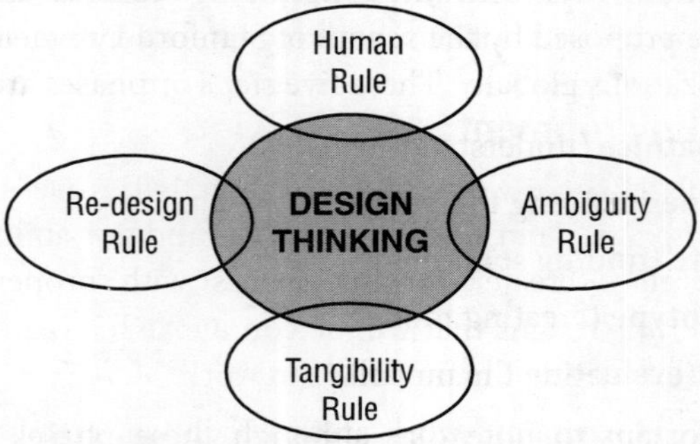

Fig.5.3: Principles of Design Thinking

Human Rule

Design thinking is basically a user-centric process and therefore all design activities are social in nature. Concerns and needs of the users are paramount. Logic alone may not work all the time.

Ambiguity Rule

Ambiguity is the quality of being open to more than one interpretation. This is inevitable in the process of design thinking. We should be able not only to see different things but also to see things differently .

Re-design Rule

No design is permanent in nature. When technology, circumstances and needs change, we may have to relook at the entire process and redesign the means of fulfilling the new requirements.

Tangibility Rule

Tangibility means easily understandable. We must make our ideas tangible so as to facilitate designers to understand them easily and communicate more effectively among themselves.

5.6 PHASES OF DESIGN THINKING

Design thinking process can be thought of as a series of steps or phases that incorporate the above principles. There are many variants of these steps in use today, varying from three to seven. All of them are very similar and embody more or less the same concepts. We consider here a **five-step** model, the one proposed by the school of Stanford University and widely used in organizations globally. These five steps or phases are as follows:

1. **Empathise** (understanding users)
2. **Define** (defining the problem)
3. **Ideate** (finding solutions)
4. **Prototype** (creating models)
5. **Test** (evaluating the models)

It is important to note that although these phases appear to be sequential, design thinking does not strictly follow a linear sequence. During the process, we may discover something new in one phase that may take us to a previous phase and repeat it. It is really an iterative process as shown in Fig.5.4.

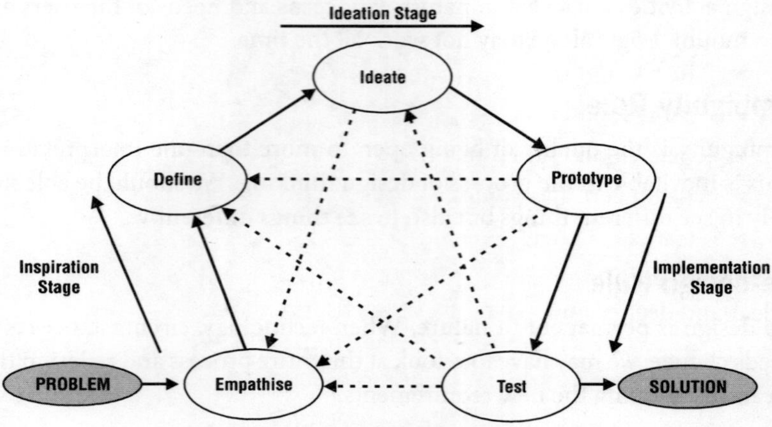

Fig.5.4: Phases of Design Thinking

Empathise

Empathise means understand and share the feeling of others. Here, others are the customers or end users of our solution, may be a product or service. The primary objective of this phase therefore is to understand the problems faced by the customers and to know their wants, needs and objectives. In short, we need to empathise with them and understand them on a psychological and emotional level.

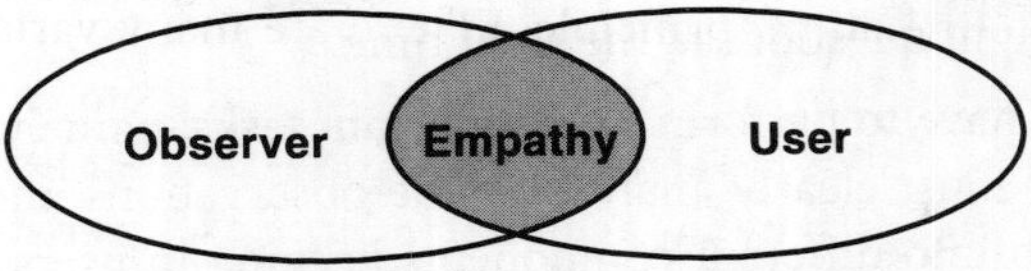

Fig.5.5: Empathising with Users

This is a requirements gathering phase which might involve interviews, observations and sometimes, even field visits. During such interviews, we must set aside our own assumptions and beliefs in order to gain insight into users and their needs.

At this stage, we must not only gather a substantial amount of information but also develop the best possible understanding of the users and the issues that underlie the development of the required solution.

There are a few qualities an observer must possess and exhibit during observations and interviews. They include:

- Be Egoless
- Be Humble
- Be Curious
- Be a Good Listener
- Be a Good Observer
- Be a Good Questioner
- Be Sincere and Honest
- Care for Others

Observers may practice using the **What-How-Why** questions to gain a clear and deeper understanding of the users and the problem.

> *"The main tenet of design thinking is empathy for the people you are trying to design for."*

—David M. Kelley

Define

It is time to put together all the information and findings we have gathered in the empathise phase and start making sense of them. The key here is to define the problem in a user-centric way.

It is said that a well-defined problem often contains its own solution. By defining the problem properly, we make it easier to understand and easier to solve. Often, problem definition is nothing more than the art of asking a few right questions at the right time.

Here, we have to perform two important tasks, namely, analysis and synthesis. We must clearly analyse all the observations and findings by breaking them into different components keeping in users' needs rather than those of the business and come out with different possible problem definitions. We must then combine all of them together (synthesis) and convert them into a coherent single statement.

Given below are some suggestions that could be useful:

- Amplify the positive aspects of the needs and views of customers
- Remove all the bad elements observed in the problem
- Critically question the assumptions if any
- Identify any other requirements not specified by the customers
- Think of a similar problem or situation existing elsewhere

The final problem statement should be user-centric, broad enough for creativity, yet specific enough to provide guidance and directions for further work.

Ideate

Ideate means generate or develop prescriptive ideas. After defining the problem in clear terms, we should now generate as many ideas as possible for potential solutions. It is a crucial stage where the creative thinking plays an important role.

How do we generate ideas? There are many ideation techniques and tools available and we may use one or more of them as situation warrants. Popular among them are brainstorming, mind mapping and role-plying. Whatever tool we use, it is important to generate as many ideas or problem solutions as possible through the process of divergent thinking.

Finally, we must narrow down 'many' to 'few' unique solution ideas using the process of convergent thinking. These selected ideas will be moved to the next phase for prototyping.

The processes of divergent and convergent thinking are illustrated in Fig.5.6.

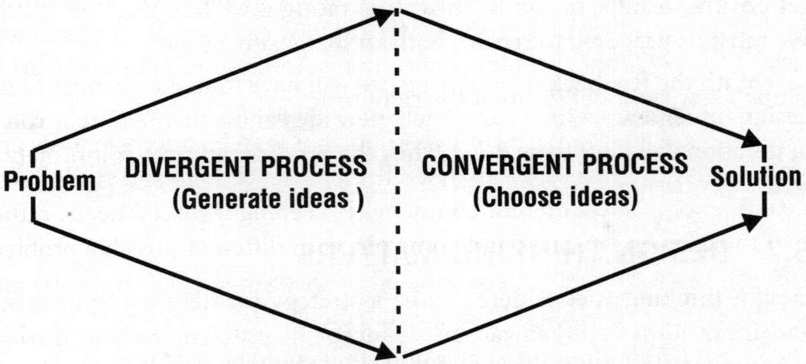

Fig.5.6: Divergent and Convergent Processes

Prototype

Prototype is a model of a product or service created for the purpose of testing and demonstrating a concept , process or product. Having narrowed our ideas down to a select few in the idea phase, we will now convert them into prototypes, that is 'scaled-down' versions of the product or concept we want to test. They must incorporate all the potential features identified in the earlier phase. This phase involves actually three tasks:

- Creation of models,
- Getting feedback, and
- Iteration.

When creating models, we must keep in mind the needs and concerns of end users. The prototypes are then tested within the team first and then with the users. All the feedbacks such as short-comings, criticisms, suggestions and appreciations are gathered and analysed carefully. To incorporate any suggestions and improvements, we may have to go back to earlier steps, namely, Empathise, Define, and Ideate.

After a series of iterations and discussions, revised or improved versions of prototypes are ready for final testing.

Test

This is the final stage of evaluation and execution. Prototypes have to be tested on real or representative users. In this stage, we must be collaborative and agile.

Testing will enable us to understand what actually works, what does not, and what needs improvements. This step can be most exciting if we get positive results, or can be most frustrating if we face negative results. We must be prepared to receive both with a positive mind.

With the feedback from testing, we will have to make changes to our design or come up with a completely new idea altogether. Another round of iteration will have to be done. Thus the process can stretch infinitely as well.

5.7 DESIGN THINKING MATTERS

Design thinking is considered to be a strategy for developing creativity and innovation in organizations. Concept of problem solving through experimentation with users makes design thinking an empathy-driven, solution-oriented methodology, rather than a business-driven, problem-oriented one. Anything that involves human interactions, may be products, services or processes can be improved through design thinking.

There are many unique features of design thinking that make it a favourite strategy among the leading business and industrial organizations. Some of the features include:

- Fosters creativity and innovation
- Follows middle-path thinking (between intuition and logic)
- Encourages human-centered, empathy-driven approach
- Supports solution-based rather than problem-based methodology
- Suitable for solving "wicked" problems
- Works very well with lean and agile thinking
- Reduces time-to-market significantly
- Yields better return on investment
- Improves customer retention and loyalty
- Can be applied across organizations

Lean and Agile Thinking

Lean thinking: It is a way of thinking that would result in delivering more value at less expense to customers. Less expense means reducing the wastage of time and efforts in performing a task. It means continuously improving the business processes to provide high levels of customer satisfaction.

The term 'lean thinking' was coined by James Womack and Daniel Jones while making an in-depth study of Toyota Production System. Lean thinking in manufacturing is an approach to thinking that focuses on minimizing waste within manufacturing processes while simultaneously maximizing the productivity.

The basic insight of lean thinking is that if we train every employee to identify resources that are wasted in terms of time, material and effort in their jobs and to improve processes by eliminating such wastes, the organization would be able deliver more value to people at less expense. Two important concepts involved in lean thinking are *continuous improvement* and *respect for people*.

Agile thinking: Agile means ability to move quickly and easily. Agile thinking is therefore a way of thinking which enables us to respond to changes or to solve problems *quickly* and *easily*. It is the ability to consciously shift our thinking style as and when the situation requires and to deliver products and services in the way customer wants and at the time customer needs them. It is a flexible and adaptive thinking approach to problem-solving and project management.

In project management, agile thinking is an iterative and incremental way of implementing things that gives an ability to respond quickly and easily to dynamic needs of the market. Agile thinking increases customer insights and encourages and appreciates value, speed, and flexibility.

Both agile and lean thinking prioritize customers as a primary goal. However, agile focuses on *quick delivery* of services to customers while lean aims at *minimizing waste* and *maximizing value* to customers.

5.8 APPLICATIONS OF DESIGN THINKING

We have just seen many different features of design thinking. Several organizations around the globe in areas such as entertainment, education, research, business, banking, management, industry, technology, communication, travel and NGOs have started applying DT extensively to improve their operational efficiency and effectiveness. As an illustration, a few examples are discussed here.

Business

Someone said, "successful businesses are making billions by recognizing the value of design thinking and integrating it into their process". An absolutely a correct statement.

Major functions of any business are creation of products and services, marketing them, and serving the clients and customers. All these processes require a company-wide focus on their customers. Businesses must recognize that it is critical to respond appropriately to the changing trends and customer behaviours. That is why many Fortune 500 companies such as Apple, Microsoft, and IBM have demonstrated the application of "design thinking" as a competitive advantage for driving their business growth.

These organizations have also realized that design thinking integrates three essential business components, namely, *desirability* of customers, *viability* at the business level, and *feasibility* for technology. Business innovation occurs at the intersection of these three components as shown in Fig.5.7.

Design thinking shifts the focus from a business-centric solution to a customer-centric solution that explores culture of people, observes how people think and behave, and gains insights into what they need. Products and services are designed around this.

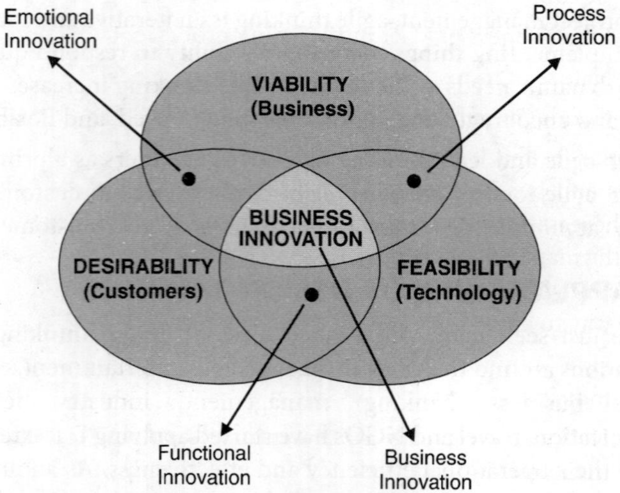

Fig.5.7: Design Thinking for Business Innovation

As stated earlier, applying design thinking to business operations results in many benefits:

- User-need based solutions
- Better return on investment(ROI)
- Improved customer retention and loyalty
- Better marketing and sales

- Fast delivery of products with better quality
- Improved competitive advantage

It is obviously clear that design thinking approach provides significant, positive changes throughout the organization. Many startup companies that adopted design thinking methodology have performed better than their counterparts.

Education

Education is an important area which attracts the attention of everyone. Education system must always be dynamic and come out often with creative solutions in order to meet the ever changing requirements of industries and society. Stakeholders in education are always concerned about not only the quality but also the relevance of education. Some important related issues are:

- Relevance of curriculum
- Adequacy of classrooms and laboratories
- Effectiveness of teaching/learning processes
- Nature of industrial collaborations
- Conducive environment for enhancing creativity

Regular feedback from stakeholders like students, parents, teachers, industries and business leaders can prove to be an effective strategy to address these issues. Here comes in the application of design thinking. DT can help the management to develop a deep understanding of stakeholders and come up with relevant and creative solutions to address these issues. A simple way to apply DT is to ask some basic questions such as:

- How can we redesign our curriculum around the needs of industries?
- How can we create a 21st century learning experience at our institute?
- How can we foster creative and innovative thinking among students?

And so on.

Information Technology

IT industries produce a lot of products and services that have direct impact on customers. It is not just enough to deploy technologies. They need to empathise with the clients and users. Acceptance of users is of paramount importance for the success of products launched. These companies must focus on the customer and delivering the best user experience possible so as to enable them to maintain competitive advantage. This is where the adoption of design thinking methodology brings wonders.

A study of IEEE, "why software fails" has identified many reasons for failure of software projects. Three reasons are related to user-centered design failure:

1. Badly defined user requirements
2. Poor communications among customers and developers
3. Stakeholder politics

Design thinking provides a simple way to hone in on such problems and provide insights that critical to success.

Today, many leading organizations are focusing on implementation of Artificial Intelligence (AI) into their applications. To ensure successful AI implementations, the organizations must first figure out why, where, and how they can apply AI to specific business problems. Design thinking can do this task wonderfully well.

Healthcare

Globally, healthcare industry is growing at a very fast rate. Both governments and private sectors are spending huge amounts of money in this area which is increasing every day. In countries like India, more than 60% of people live in villages and more than one-fourth of population is below poverty line. Some major concerns of healthcare experts and government officials are:

- How to improve the quality of healthcare
- How to reduce the cost of healthcare
- How to make healthcare available to rural and remote areas
- How to improve the quality of patient care and experience in hospitals
- How to meet the special needs of women and children
- How to control or prevent the spread of an epidemic like COVID-19

Healthcare systems must address not only these issues but also require continuous innovation to meet the needs of patients and healthcare providers. Design thinking can be used as a strategy to address these challenges and to enhance innovation, efficiency, and effectiveness of healthcare systems by focusing on the users.

Many hospitals across the globe have been using design thinking to improve their systems and services. A recent study has shown that DT interventions have been greatly successful in enhancing user satisfaction and system effectiveness.

Government

A government is an umbrella body that governs almost everything in a country-from controlling large companies to guiding ordinary people on the roads. Since governments are established by the people and for the people, they undertake numerous developmental projects, launch many welfare schemes, and provide policies and guidelines on many aspects of governing the people. Some notable areas that have direct impact on people are education, health, sanitation, agriculture, banking, transport, public distribution, law and order and taxation. Some of the policy issues address increasingly complex social problems like reservations, population control, poverty alleviation and education for all. The main focus in all these policies, projects and activities is the *people.* That is, all of them are human-centric.

The design thinking, a human-centric process which involves concepts like

- Understanding and empathising users,
- Defining the problem,
- Generating innovative solutions, and
- Experimenting through prototyping and testing

is therefore very much relevant to decision making in government. In fact, policy makers may be using some of the aspects of design thinking in their daily functioning, without really knowing they are doing it. A conscious use of design thinking can be incredibly a powerful approach to help policy makers improve public services and make government more responsive to its citizens, especially when facing complex, wicked problems.

Some of the potential benefits include the following:

- Improve service delivery in terms of reach and effectiveness

- Improve program efficiency in terms cost and relevance
- Build capacity and work across various departments

In every department of the government, there is immense scope for improving their working efficiency and thereby bettering the outreach to people. User interaction and user experience are very relevant and important for government policy makers.

One of the design consultants rightly said:

> *" Government policy makers and administrators would be well served by getting trained in design thinking methodology and using its principles in their work that will put citizens first in policies and programmes."*

5.9 ATTRIBUTES OF DESIGN THINKING LEADERS

Technology is changing fast, so also the needs of customers. Business leaders are therefore under constant pressure to produce new and innovative products and services that would meet the interests and needs of customers. In the process of looking for new methods, many of them have started adopting design thinking as an approach to address their problems. Design thinking is not just a magic tool that can be simply applied to solve a problem. It is a long iterative process that involves customers as well as people in the organization. It is therefore imperative that business leaders imbibe certain qualities in order to implement DT successfully. Listed below are twelve attributes that every aspiring design thinking leader should possess.

1. Curious thinker
2. Empathic thinker
3. Collaborative worker
4. Optimistic thinker
5. Keen experimentalist
6. Willingness to learn from failures
7. Integrative thinker
8. Communicative thinker
9. Embraces ambiguity

10. Believes in prototyping
11. Good observer and listener
12. Accepts others insights

> *"Design must reflect the practical and aesthetic in business but above all... good design must primarily serve the people."*
>
> —THOMAS J. WATSON

5.10 REVIEW QUESTIONS

1. What is design thinking? Explain its three essential components.
2. Describe a few situations where design thinking can be used successfully.
3. List some important features of design thinking.
4. Explain wicked-problems with an example.
5. What do you mean by critical success factors? Explain the four critical success factors that are associated with design thinking.
6. Enlighten the four principles that govern the design thinking process.
7. Describe briefly the five-step model of design thinking.
8. What is the relevance of divergent and convergent processes in design thinking?
9. What is agile thinking? How is it different from lean thinking?
10. Describe two examples of application of design thinking in industries.
11. Enumerate important traits of a design thinker.

6 Ethical Thinking

> *"In a world of ethical complexity, leaders need to learn clear and coherent ethical thinking"*

6.1 INTRODUCTION

Ethics is a very complex and intricate concept for anyone to easily understand. Most people appear to be confused when we ask, "what is ethics?" In one of the seminars on 'Business Ethics', participants were asked to define ethics. Some replies were:

"Doing things according to law."

"Being transparent in doing things."

"Not cheating others in business."

"Behaving as per the society norms."

"Respecting others in our work."

"Working according to our feelings."

Who is right? Apparently, everyone seems to be correct. It is very difficult to pin point what exactly ethics is.

This reminds us a famous parable, "Elephant and the blind men". Once upon a time, there lived six blind men in a village. One day, the villagers told them that there is an elephant in the village. The blind men had no idea of an elephant and decided to touch it and understand how an elephant looks like. Every one of them touched the elephant.

" Elephant is a huge wall " said the first man.

" It is a big hand fan " said the second.

" Elephant is a pillar " said the one who touched the leg.

" It is a solid pipe " said the fourth man happily.

" Oh, it is like a big branch of a tree " said the who touched the trunk.

" No, no, it is a rope " said the last man who was holding the tail.

They started arguing and each one of them said he is correct. A wise village man standing nearby saw them almost fighting. He calmly explained them, " All of you are right. The reason for different opinion is that each one of you touched the different part of the elephant. Actually the elephant has all those features." There was no more fight. They felt happy that they were all right.

The moral of the story is that there may be some truth in what someone says. Ethics is like the elephant.

Look at the answers by the participants to the question, "what is ethics?". In some answers we may find truth and in some other we may not, because they may have different perspectives which we may not agree to the same extent. Perhaps, we might say, "May be you have your reasons". While one's subjective experience is true, it may not be the totality of truth.

Doing things according to law is not exactly being ethical. The law may often incorporate ethical standards, but many a times laws can deviate from what is ethical. For example, awarding death sentence for a murderer may be right as per the law but cannot be considered as ethical. Similarly, laws on reservations in education, employments and promotions certainly deviate from what is ethical.

Following society norms is again not necessarily being ethical. Although most people in a society follow certain standards that are considered to be ethical, their behavior at times can deviate from ethical practices. For instance, corruption may be a way of life in some society. In some places, predatory money lending is a common practice.

Another wrong thinking among people is to equate ethics with their feelings. Persons acting according to their feelings often deviate from what is right. They are guided by their emotions rather than logic.

What, then, ethics is?

6.2 WHAT IS ETHICS?

> *"Ethics is the activity of a man directed to secure the inner perfection of his personality."*

—ALBERT SCHWEITZER

Ethics refers to a set of standards that prescribe what people are supposed to do in terms of rights, obligations, fairness, and benefits to society. Whenever a situation arises for making a choice, ethics guide us in deciding the right choice. Ethics is therefore a basic requirement for everybody. It enables us to decide a course of action. Without it, perhaps our actions would be random and aimless; sometimes, they may be even worthless.

Therefore, ethics, at its simplest form, is a system of moral principles that govern people's behavior and actions and aid them in making right decisions. The core principles of ethics would include:

1. **Honesty** (Being honest in all our communications and actions)
2. **Integrity** (Maintaining personal integrity in our thoughts, words and actions)
3. **Transparency** (Being open-minded and honest in all our actions)
4. **Trustworthiness** (Being reliable, dependable and honest)
5. **Loyalty** (Being loyal to the people and organizations we work with)
6. **Fairness** (Trying to be fair and just in all our activities)
7. **Respect** (Treating everyone with courtesy and respect)
8. **Caring** (Demonstrating compassion and concern for others)
9. **Responsibility** (Fulfillment of assigned tasks and taking responsibility for actions)
10. **Accountability** (Being accountable for all actions and decisions)
11. **Equality** (Treating everyone in the same way without any bias or discrimination)
12. **Justice** (Ensuring that each receives what he deserves)

Application of ethical principles depends on the situation in which a person encounters and varies from one person to another.

In addition to ethics, values and morals can also influence thinking process considerably. See Fig.6.1.

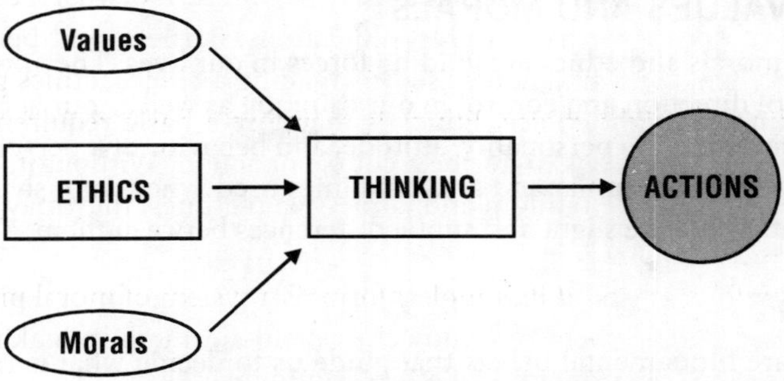

Fig.6.1: Process of Ethical Thinking

Ethics emphasizes the responsibility and capability of people to come to their own conclusions through ethical thinking and reasoning, and determine which principles are relevant in a particular situation. Ethics imposes reasonable obligations for us to refrain from hurting others, stealing, murder, fraud, and sometimes an obligation to help others. Ethics also includes virtues of honesty, loyalty, and integrity.

If we want to think and live ethically, we must continuously review our own beliefs and conduct, and strive to ensure that we live up to the standards that are reasonable and evidence-based. Most philosophers say that the best way to achieve our fullest potential is by practicing ethical thinking and reasoning regularly.

6.3 WHY ETHICS?

Ethics guides human life. The term is derived from the Greek word 'ethos' which means character, habit, custom or disposition. Human beings often behave irrationally. They follow their 'gut feelings' even when their head suggests differently. However, ethics can guide them and put them on the correct path. Following are some of the benefits of ethics:

- Helps to lead a happy life
- Provides a moral framework
- Helps in solving conflicts
- Eliminates confusions in decision making
- Could provide several right answers
- Encourages compassion
- Provides moral strength
- Helps to gain credibility

6.4 VALUES AND MORALS

Values, morals and ethics are guiding forces in our lives. They provide us a sense of direction and control in our thinking as well as our actions. All the three define the personality, attitude, and behavior of a person. While they appear to be similar and are sometimes used synonymously, they are different. There are slight and subtle differences between them.

Values

Values are fundamental beliefs that guide us to decide what is right and wrong and what is just and fair. They also tell us which are more or less important, which is useful when we trade off certain things. Values are normally influenced by family background, culture, community, religion, etc.

Some examples of values are honesty, justice, respect, patriotism, love, compassion, etc. Values are personal to individuals and can vary from person to person.

Let us consider a person preparing for an exam. If his value system is strongly founded upon honesty, he would not think of cheating in the exam hall for the sake of scoring good marks. On the other hand, if he valued success over honesty, then he would not mind using any malpractice in the exam to achieve desired result.

Morals

Morals are values that are imposed from outside and meant to guide us in our day to day work. They are codes of conduct that tell us what is right and what is wrong. Morals mostly come from society and religion and therefore can vary according to different cultures and religion. Some moral principles are loyalty, patience, truth, generosity, freedom, charity, etc.

A person who knows the difference between right and wrong and chooses the right is moral. A person who chooses the right one in spite of it being a dangerous choice is ethical.

Values vs Morals

Consider a person working in a medical store. His wife is in need of a life-saving medicine which he could not afford. He has access to the medicine in the store. If he wants to save his wife he must steal the medicine. His core values tell him stealing is wrong. But his morality tells him to save his wife. What should he do? He is facing a situation what is known as a 'moral dilemma'.

He may choose to steal the medicine (wrong thing as judged by his morals) for saving his wife (right reason as judged by his values). Many a times, we end up in doing wrong things for right purposes.

Values, morals and ethics together have a direct impact on our attitude and behavior as shown in Fig.62. They could help us make the right decisions by providing proper guidelines.

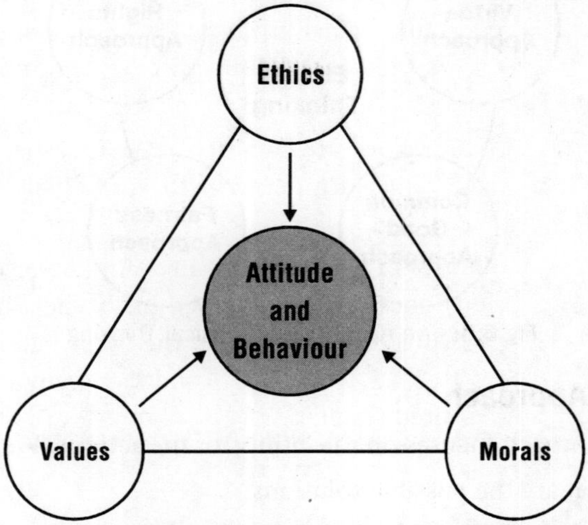

Fig.6.2: Triangle of Impact on Attitude and Behavior

6.5 FIVE WAYS OF ETHICAL THINKING

Almost every day we face ethical issues. They put our values and morals into question. Resolving ethical issues require a careful analysis of all the facts involved. Moral issues might create controversies if we ignore any facts. There two fundamental questions in using ethical standards in our thinking process.

What is the basis of using our ethical standards?

How do we apply those standards to a particular issue?

There are five ways or approaches available for addressing these questions. They are:

- Utilitarian Approach

- Rights Approach
- Fairness Approach
- Common Good Approach
- Virtue Approach

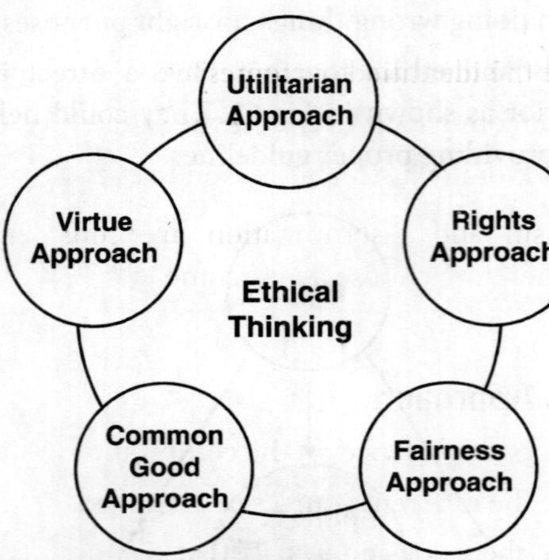

Fig.6.3: Five Approaches to Ethical Thinking

Utilitarian Approach

Utilitarian approach focuses on the 'utility' of the actions. We must ask:

- What are the possible solutions?
- What are the benefits or harms of each one?
- Which one will provide the best utility for all concerned?

The problem must be analyzed from several different perspectives before arriving at possible solutions. We must choose the one that has the best utility value for everyone concerned.

Rights Approach

This one places greater emphasis on the rights of the people.

- What are the rights of the people involved?
- What are the possible actions?
- Which action will safeguard those rights?

We must appreciate that people have certain moral rights and they have the ability to make their own decisions. The rights might include rights to privacy, rights to truth, rights not to be harmed, etc. The solution must guarantee these rights of the people involved.

Fairness Approach

This approach tells us to treat everybody equally without undue discrimination.

- What are the identified outcomes?
- Which outcome treats everyone the same way?
- Is there a morally justifiable reason to exclude someone?

Both favoritism and discrimination are considered unjust and wrong. We must therefore choose an outcome that is fair to all the people concerned.

Common Good Approach

This approach places importance on the community as a whole.

- What are the different courses of action possible?
- What are the values and goals that community members hold in common?
- Which course of action promotes the common good?

These questions help us drive our choice to decide the right course of action that would benefit all members of the community.

Virtue Approach

Virtue approach emphasizes our character (virtue) as the element of ethical thinking.

- What are our principal virtues? (honesty, loyalty, fairness, courage, generosity, etc)
- Is the action reflective of the kind of person we are or want to be?
- Will it promote the kind of character we value?

We must remember that no approach or method guarantees an automatic solution to ethical problems. They are basically meant to identify important moral and ethical considerations. It is for us to deliberate carefully on various moral issues and decide on a course of action that would enable us to develop moral virtues in ourselves and our communities.

6.6 EXAMPLES OF ETHICAL ISSUES

Ethical issues arise when we face conflicting situations where we have to choose between two alternative outcomes, right (ethical) and wrong (unethical). Actions or decisions that affect others will always have an ethical dimension. Ethical issues may be related to individuals (personal ethics), profession (professional ethics), business (business ethics) or society (social ethics). Ethical issues may be challenging if no guidelines or precedents are available. Some examples of ethical issues are listed below.

Social Ethics

- Should animals have rights?
- Is death penalty an acceptable punishment?
- Can we make wearing helmet mandatory?
- Can we make prohibition compulsory?
- Can we permit social discrimination ?
- Can we ban certain social media activities?
- Is it right for a country to wage war on another country?
- Is it right to encourage religious conversions?
- Is it right to support caste-based reservations?
- Is it right to ban caste or religion based politics?

Business Ethics

- Selling outdated medicine
- Selling duplicate products
- Selling adulterated items
- Hoarding and black-marketing
- Forging records in order to avoid taxes
- Not paying fair wages to employees
- Paying bribes to get things done through unfair means
- Unfair claims in advertisements
- Employing child labour
- Not adhering to regulatory guidelines
- Unhealthy competitive practices

Professional Ethics

- Not being truthful to the profession
- Not being loyal to the employer
- Not taking responsibility for the actions and consequences
- Misusing resources of the organization, like money, material and time
- Disobeying laws and guidelines
- Stealing and misusing money, data and information
- Ignoring the organizational goals and objectives
- Harassing or victimizing coworkers or subordinates
- Cheating customers and vendors
- Not being truthful to the employer
- Not committing full potential to the work
- Not being transparent in communications and work
- Trying to help competitors
- Putting personal goals above organizational goals
- Not cooperating with coworkers
- Refuse to upgrade knowledge and skill.

Personal Ethics

- Cheating a friend for something
- Breaking a queue to get a ticket
- Copying in examinations
- Speaking lies to achieve something
- Giving wrong reasons to get leave from employer
- Trying to get some undue benefits from others
- Hiding truth from others
- Not paying taxes that are due
- Trying to use unfair means to win a competition
- Using personal powers to get something done against law
- Making a promise that cannot be kept
- Making excuses for the mistakes committed

- Misrepresenting information for personal gains
- Not taking responsibility for own actions and consequences
- Not helping the needy and deserving people
- Hurting the feelings of people of other communities and religions

6.7 ETHICAL DILEMMA

Ethical dilemmas (also known as moral dilemmas) are situations in which there is a choice to be made between two options, when both of them are not ethically acceptable. We are not sure of our choice. In such situations, we may feel ourselves being pulled by competing ethical demands. Our decision in either way be lead to blames and criticisms.

Let us consider the case of a young man working in the Army. While he was on leave at his village to attend his ailing mother, he was called by an order to report for duty to fight against an intruding enemy army in the border. Now there is an ethical dilemma before him, to save the mother or to save the mother land, his country.

Some people may say that someone else can take care of her. But he knew that his mother lived only for him and that any thought of his death in the war would make her lose all her hopes in life. He also knew that fighting for the country is a greater cause.

Ethical dilemmas are basically a clash of moral values. A decision either way may violate some value that is close to us. For example, you and your close friend are working for an organization. One day, you come to know that your friend has passed on some secret data to some other organization. Now, you face an ethical question embodied by two important values, honesty and loyalty. Your honesty says you should inform your employer about the fraud and get him punished, but your loyalty says you should not let your longtime friend down.

Similar ethical dilemma situations arise when doctors and nurses attend to the patients of COVID-19 or when a fire service officer tries to save someone inside a building under fire.

In all these instances, our values play an important role. Ultimately, what we choose to value most will play a significant role in deciding our action. We come across many ethical dilemmas in real life. Some examples are listed below.

1. Doing Personal Business at Workplace

You are working in an organization. You have decided to do some side business to enhance your monthly income. You often meet your business people at working hours, use office computers and telephones for your personal work and entertain your personal guests at office expenses. There is clearly an ethical issue.

You not only misuse company time and resources for your personal benefit but also cause loss to the company. It is clearly an abuse of your office to conduct personal business and therefore it is unethical.

2. Professional Conflict

You are an engineer in a processing industry. Management wants to introduce a new processing technology to enhance productivity and thereby profit. You as a process engineer is aware that the use of new technology would cause serious environmental pollution and likely to affect the health of thousands of people living around the industry.

Will you implement the new technology as required by the management? Or will you resist the use of new technology to save the life of thousands of people?

The ethical dilemma is fairly clear.

3. Employee Loyalty

You are a marketing executive in an organization. You are looking for a career change. You are attending an interview with one of the competitors. You are offered a huge salary with lots of perks, provided if you share the customer data base of your present employer.

Sharing company's information with a competitor is unethical. But the offer is so exciting that you do not want to miss it. What will you do?

The ethical issue is trustworthiness. Even if you join the new company, will they trust you?

4. Physician's Dilemma

You are a physician in a reputed hospital. You are the consulting doctor to a patient who is on life supporting systems. You know that the patient is suffering from discomfort and severe pain without any hope of survival. Many may think it is time to withdraw life support and let nature take its course. You may also feel the same thing. But the patient's family insists that you do everything possible to keep the patient alive.

How will you address this situation? There is a conflict between professional ethics and personal opinion.

5. Causing an Accident

You are driving car on a national highway at high speed. Suddenly you realized that your car has hit a motorcycle going on your left and the motorcycle and rider have fallen on the ground. You also noticed that no one is around the place to report the incident.

Will you stop your car and try to help the victim? Or will you proceed without stopping since no one has seen the incidence? Stopping and helping might lead to police case.

Ignoring situation may be the easiest solution but is it ethically appropriate?

6.8 CAUSES OF UNETHICAL PRACTICES

Many organizations and individuals resort to unethical activities and practices due to tough competition and greed for money. There are a number of other factors which contribute to unethical practices. Some of them are:

1. Time pressure

When people work under pressure of time, they tend to ignore the ethical ways of doing things in order to achieve targets.

2. Unrealistic goals

When we fix goals or targets that are not achievable easily, we are forced to follow certain unethical practices.

3. Lack of transparency

Lack of transparency will encourage the use of unethical means among employees.

4. Over obedience

In the process of pleasing the boss or authorities, people overlook ethical norms.

5. Over confidence

People generally think that they are more ethical than others and therefore tend to be happy with their moral values. Such overconfidence often leads them to make unethical decisions.

6. Over government regulations

Unnecessary regulations and controls from regulatory agencies force people to adopt unethical means to please authorities.

7. Absence of ethical norms

One important reason for prevalence of unethical practices in organizations is the absence of any Code of Conduct or Ethical norms. There is nothing to check whether an act is ethical or not.

8. Environmental factors

The operating environment can facilitate unethical behavior if proper ethical framework is not in place.

6.9 SOURCES OF ETHICS

Every individual has a set of ethical principles which that person uses to distinguish between morally acceptable or morally unacceptable behaviors. We as individuals draw ethical principles from a variety of sources. Since the sources may be different for different individuals, their ethical thinking may also differ for a particular situation.

What are those sources? The sources may be childhood upbringing, work experience, society, law, religion and even friends. Fig.6.4 illustrates different types sources from where individuals usually imbibe ethical principles.

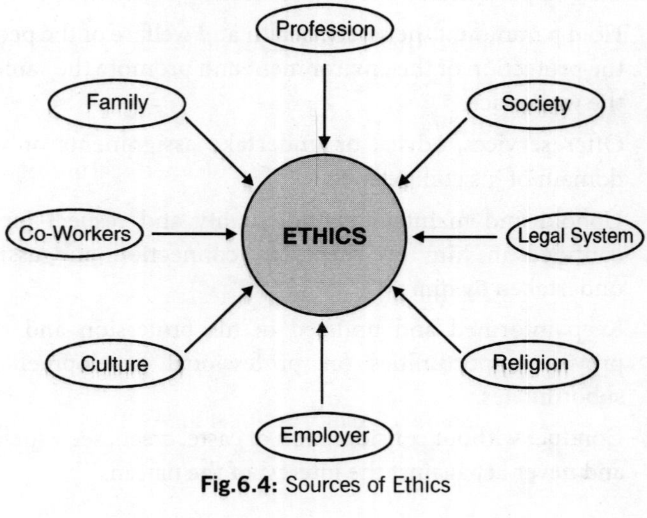

Fig.6.4: Sources of Ethics

Family

For every one of us, the primary source of moral values is our family. We learn at a very early stage of our life, what is right and what is wrong from the teachings and actions of our parents and grandparents. Even close family relatives may contribute to our character development.

Coworkers

Later in life when we start working, we receive a lot of opinions and views from coworkers in the work place about whether what we have been saying and doing are bad, good and meaningful. Many a time, such feedbacks greatly help us refine our ethical thinking and behavior. Friends also play similar roles in shaping our moral behavior.

Profession

Every profession has its own set of ethical norms that are to be followed strictly by those practicing that profession. Perhaps, the 'Code of Conduct' prescribed by professional associations provide us the most direct and explicit sources of daily ethical guidance. For example:

An engineer shall:

1. Practice his profession with integrity, dignity and honour and follow the best traditions of the profession with conscience.
2. Be aware of the principles of sustainable engineering and ensure their implementation in all engineering activities.
3. Hold paramount the safety, health and welfare of the people and the protection of the environment and promote the same within the workplace.
4. Offer services, advice or undertake assignments only in the domain of his competence.
5. Uphold and maintain confidentiality and respect for secrets confided in him by clients in connection any assignment undertaken by him.
6. Keep informed and updated in his profession and strive to provide opportunities for professional development of his subordinates.
7. Conduct without consideration of caste, creed, sect, social status and never act against the interest of the nation.

8. Not directly or indirectly injure the reputation of another engineer.
9. Present clearly to all concerned the possible consequences which may arise out of his actions while undertaking an engineering assignment.
10. Shall reject any kind of offer that may involve unfair practice or any act that may damage reputation or cause any financial loss to his employer.

Employer

All industrial and business organizations prescribe a set of conduct rules and guidelines to be followed by their employees in their daily work. In fact, some organizations have set up 'Ethical Centres' and 'Ethical Help Lines' to address ethical issues faced by their employees.

Culture

Culture refers to the rules, customs, and standards followed by generations after generations as guidelines for appropriate behavior. The human civilization is cumulative of cultural experience that an individual passes through during his lifetime.

Society

Society refers to a group people living together with a common territory. Society normally defines guidelines and norms for the ethical conduct of its members. Society has always had its share of flaws and false standards.

Legal System

Legal systems formulate the conduct rules to be followed by the citizens of the state. These rules and procedures confirm to the ethical behavior of everyone in every business. However, there are situations where a solution may be legally right but ethically wrong.

Religion

There are numerous religions followed by people. Each religion talks about the nature of right and wrong in daily walk of life. Religious teachings have very strong impact on them and therefore are deeply rooted in their behavior, in both personal and business situations.

6.10 ETHICAL THINKING FRAMEWORK

Most often, many actions implemented in business, industry or government are not ethically acceptable to everyone concerned. We call such actions as unethical decisions. What are ethical decisions and how can we make them?

Ethical decisions are those that are based on sound ethical principles and enhance the well-being of all concerned. Making good ethical decisions require an in-depth understanding of ethical issues and the ability to explore various options and considerations that would impact our choice of action. As illustrated in Fig.6.5, a prerequisite for a good ethical decision making is a good ethical reasoning power, which in turn requires a good ethical thinking.

Fig.6.5: Ethical Chain

The Framework

The process of ethical thinking that is necessary to make ethical decisions may be considered as an iterative 6-Step Thinking Model as depicted in Fig.6.6. Six steps are:

1. **Identification** (Identifying the ethical issue)
2. **Comprehension** (Comprehending relevant facts)
3. **Analysis** (Analysing different options)
4. **Selection** (Choosing the best option)
5. **Reflection** (Reflecting on the decision)
6. **Modification** (Effecting any change, if needed)

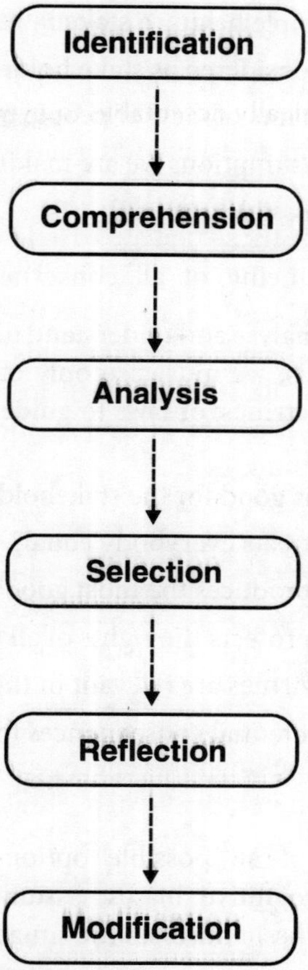

Fig.6.6: Ethical Thinking Framework

Identification

We must first identify and understand the ethical issue(s) involved properly.

- What are the different types of ethical issues involved?
- What is the primary ethical issue we want to focus on?

Comprehension

Before proceeding further, we need to gather as many relevant facts as possible. We must ask questions like, who, what, why, and how.

- What are the crucial facts of the issue?
- How are the various facts connected?

- Who are the people having a stake in the outcome?
- Why are they considered as stake holders?
- What are the points of view of people involved?
- What are the assumptions we are making?
- What are the possible options?

Analysis

This step requires us to analyse and understand different options available. In the process of analysis, we must use only ethical principles and not social rules, religious doctrines, or laws to guide our thinking. Following questions may guide us:

- Which option is good for the stakeholders as a whole?
- Which option treats everybody equal?
- Which option produces the most good?
- Which option protects the rights of all parties?
- What specific virtues are relevant in the situation?
- What are the potential consequences for the affected parties?

Selection

After careful analysis of all possible options and also taking into consideration of any cognitive biases, assumptions and suggestions, choose an option which best addresses the situation.

Reflection

We must now act on implementation of our choice.

- What consequences are likely to follow if we implement the option?
- What will happen if we choose other options?
- What are the reactions from stakeholders?

Modification

Based on the answers to the above questions, we may change or modify our option appropriately.

Thinking ethically and making ethical decisions require a deep understanding of the ethical implications of problems and solutions.

It also needs practice. A framework for ethical thinking will certainly enhance our ability to arrive at a better ethical solution.

6.11 QUALITIES NEEDED BY ETHICAL THINKERS

To think, act, and reason ethically, we must understand and apply certain ethical concepts or ideas to the ethical issue under consideration. To be ethical basically means that we must act in such a way that it does good (and avoids harm) to the people. We must continuously monitor our own feelings, thoughts and actions. We must learn to see and appreciate the 'good' in our enemies and the 'evil' in ourselves. According to the American social scientist William Graham Sumner,

> *"The feeling that we are good and others are evil is never true."*

We are all a mixture of both. The list below suggests some important qualities that are needed to be practiced by persons who would like to be called ethical thinkers themselves.

Being Fair and Forthright

Understanding, Unbiased, Impartial, Equitable, Dispassionate, objective, Honest, Loyal, Truthful, Faithful, Trustworthy

Helping Others

Generous, Unselfish, Humanitarian, Charitable, Benevolent, Altruistic, Compassionate, Merciful, Sympathetic, Empathetic, Considerate, Forgiving.

Dealing with People

Courteous, Respectful, Forbearing, Tolerant, Friendly, Cordial, Obliging, Warm hearted, Open-minded, Evenhanded, Gracious, Upright

6.12 UNIVERSAL PRINCIPLES OF ETHICS

Basic concept of ethics is that none of our actions should harm others. Therefore all the principles of ethics are derived from the Maxim 'care and compassion'. These principles are generic in nature and not prescriptive rules. No nation, no religion, and no ethnic group are against care and compassion and therefore these principles are common for people and all nations. If we want to live ethically, then we must apply these principles judiciously in everyday life.

We can group these ethical principles into three categories:

1. Personal Ethics
2. Professional Ethics
3. Global Ethics

These categories overlap each other as shown in Fig.6.7.

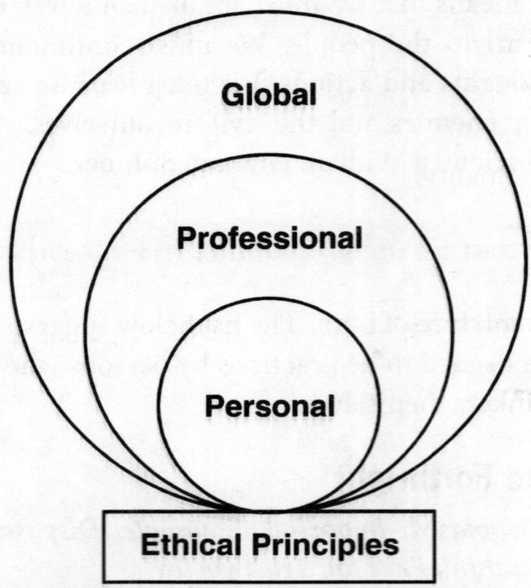

Fig.6.7: Three Categories of Ethical Principles

Personal Ethics

Personal ethics is a set of moral values that an individual in any society might use to decide what is right and wrong and what is good and bad. Personal ethics is important to produce good citizens and better leaders that would help create better societies.

Principles of personal ethics typically include but not limited to:

- Concern for others (altruistic)
- Respect for others
- Generous and charitable
- Loyal and trustworthy
- Honest and truthful
- Being fair and forthright
- Law abiding

Professional Ethics

When we become professionals in fields like engineering, medicine, law, accountancy, journalism, etc., we need to abide by certain additional level of ethical responsibility which a particular profession warrants.

Principles of professional ethics would generally include:

- Integrity
- Objectivity
- Transparency
- Accountability
- Confidentiality
- Responsiveness
- Diligence
- Faithfulness
- Willingness to learning

Global Ethics

With increasing liberalization and globalization of education, business and industrial activities, world is becoming a global village. Although we act locally, it is becoming increasingly important for us to think globally. It is therefore imperative for us to follow certain ethical values that are globally acceptable. While both the personal and professional ethics are valid globally, we, as global citizens, need to adopt some additional ethical concepts.

Principles of global ethics include:

- Respect for human race
- Social responsibility
- Reverence for other cultures
- Reverence for world peace
- Concern for environment
- Concern for sustainability
- Abiding global justice

These set of principles may appear to overlap at times. We must judiciously apply one or more of them depending upon the circumstances.

6.13 REVIEW QUESTIONS

1. Define ethics. What are the core principles of ethics?
2. How ethics matters in life?
3. Distinguish between values and morals. How do they contribute to ethical thinking?
4. What are the different approaches available for ethical decision making?
5. How does Rights Approach differ from Fairness Approach?
6. Compare Common Good Approach with Utilitarian Approach.
7. 'Virtue Approach emphasizes one's character as the element of ethical thinking.' Explain?
8. State a few examples of professional ethics. How do they differ from personal ethics?
9. What is business ethics? How does it differ from social ethics?
10. What is ethical dilemma? Discuss an ethical dilemma you faced in your personal experience.
11. What are the factors that are responsible for unethical behavior of a person?
12. 1How do employers or co-workers influence ethical behavior of a person?
13. 'Our family is the primary source of ethical values.' Comment critically.
14. Discuss briefly the framework of ethical thinking.
15. What is global ethics? How is it relevant today?

7 Systems Thinking

> *"All things appear and disappear because of causes and conditions. Nothing ever exists entirely alone; everything is in relation to everything else."*
>
> —THE BUDDHA

7.1 INTRODUCTION

We use the words system and thinking very often in our daily life. Look at the following statements:

"My system is not ok today."

"The computer system was down yesterday."

"I don't think, water distribution system is working well."

"CBSE system in India is very good."

"We must change the system of working in our office."

We are also part of many systems like our family, our community, our organization and government. Daily, we do interact with systems like banks, government departments, super markets, etc. But very rarely, we try to understand the details of these systems, how they work and how to improve their performance, if we so desire.

Systems thinking is a powerful approach for understanding the nature of why systems are the way they are, and how to go about improving their performance. Systems thinking is essentially the system of thinking about systems. Systems thinking provide us a number of benefits:

- Understand the challenges associated with change
- Fix the problems that never seem to go away
- Explore new business opportunities

- Improve the failing systems
- Design new and improved systems

With the ever increasing technological changes and challenges, our youth and workforce will need to become increasingly "system-wise" in order to keep pace with ever changing complexity of systems. It is said that systems thinking is one of the key competencies for the 21st century.

7.2 WHAT IS SYSTEMS THINKING?

Common problem solving techniques normally focus on the problems rather than the whole ecosystem where the problems really exist. Due global challenges, some of the problems are becoming more and more complex in nature and we can no longer consider them as simple or linear problems. Albert Einstein said,

> *"The problems cannot be solved using the same level of thinking that created them."*

This is where the systems thinking comes in. Systems thinking tends to focus on the whole ecosystem rather than the problem itself.

Systems thinking is an approach to holistic thinking where we think of a system as a whole rather than considering different parts individually. Holistic thinking takes into account the interrelationships of things rather than things themselves and changing patterns rather than static events.

Systems thinkers are therefore required to have a clear understanding of the linkages, interactions and interdependence of the elements that make up the system and how they affect the behavior of the whole system. To put it simply, the goal of systems thinking is to systematically discover the system's dynamics, working principles, purpose and constraints. This would enable the systems thinkers to suggest any changes or improvements, when needed.

It is therefore imperative that systems thinkers need to learn a new methodology and develop a particular way of looking at the systems and the world.

> *"System thinking is a discipline for seeing wholes. It is a framework for seeing interrelationships rather than things, for seeing 'patterns of change' rather than static 'snapshots'."*

—PETER SENGE

7.3 WHAT IS A SYSTEM?

A system may be defined as a network of interconnected, interacting, and interdependent (3Is) parts that form a unified whole in order to perform certain specified function. The key point to remember is that all the parts are interrelated and interdependent in some way and they are collectively responsible for the proper functioning of the system. Each part has a function to perform. These parts are called 'elements' in systems theory. In Fig.7.1, the elements A, B, C, and D are interconnected and interdependent and can considered as a system.

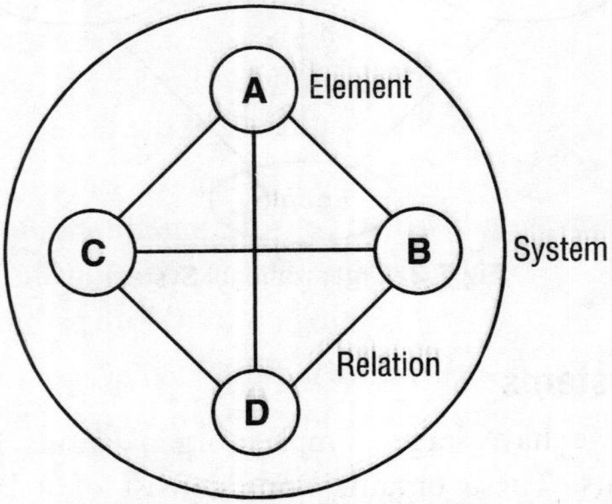

Fig.7.1: Representation of a System

An element is the most basic unit within the model of the system. It is simply a structure with possibly a function. We consider an element as a black box meaning that we do not bother to see what it is made of or how it works.

Consider a group of elements that are not interconnected and do not work together. Such a group is 'not' considered as a system. It is usually called a 'set' or a 'collection'.

Some examples of a system are:

- Computer systems

- Colleges and schools
- City corporations
- Super markets
- Factories and business organizations
- Energy systems like solar
- Transport systems
- Human body

A model of an organizational system is illustrated in Fig.7.2.

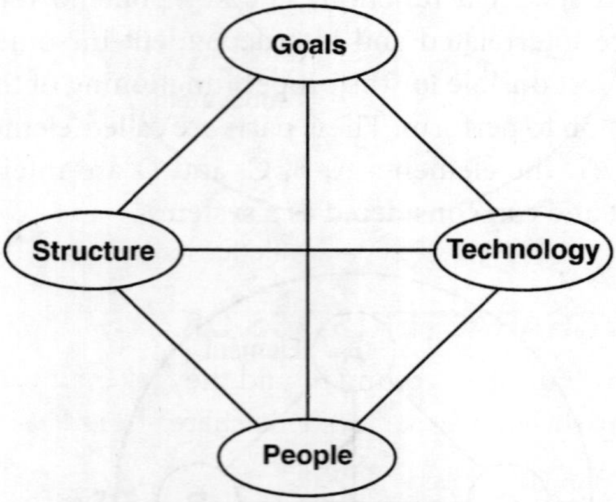

Fig.7.2: Organizational System

System of Systems

Many a time, we have large complex organizations like universities and governments. These organizations consist of a large number of independent systems within themselves. Such an organization is known as 'system of systems'. United Nations, European Union, Indian Railways, Microsoft Corporation and Anna University are typical examples of system of systems.

Subsystems

In some cases, large number of elements may be grouped into a few smaller systems known as subsystems. Therefore, a subsystem is a set of elements which make up a system. For example, the braking system in a car is a subsystem of a broader system, the car. Fig.7.3 shows three subsystems, A, B, and C, each containing three elements.

If we consider the car as a system, then transportation system which includes the car can be considered as a system of systems.

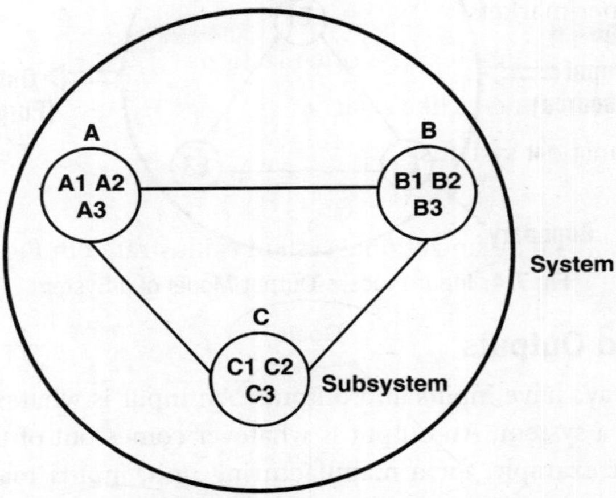

Fig.7.3: System with Subsystems

7.4 BASIC CHARACTERISTICS OF SYSTEMS

We have systems indeed all around us and they take many different forms. In spite of many differences, all systems share some basic characteristics among them.

1. Input (source) from environment
2. Process (function)
3. Output (purpose) into environment
4. Maintain stability through feedback
5. Maintain an internal steady-state (called *homeostasis*)
6. Display *emergent* properties
7. Have boundaries

All elements must be present for a system to carry out its purpose optimally. The order of arrangement of elements also affects its performance. Systems stop functioning when an element is removed or changed significantly.

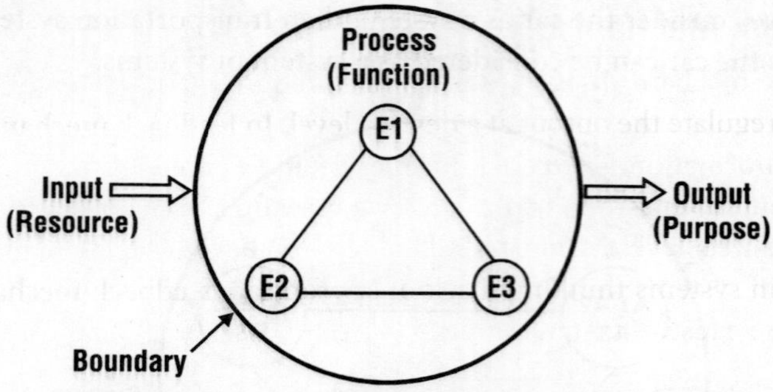

Fig.7.4: Input-Process-Output Model of a System

Inputs and Outputs

Systems always have inputs and outputs. An input is whatever resources we put into a system. An output is whatever comes out of the system as a result. For example, for a manufacturing unit, inputs may be money, materials, labour, etc. and output may be finished products. Input-Process-Output model of a system is depicted in Fig.7.4.

Processing

Resources that are inputted are processed within the system. A process is a series of actions performed on the input in order to achieve a specified result known as the output. Systems use certain instructions and procedures as to how to transform the given inputs into outputs. All the elements in the system get involved in the processing activity.

All systems use some logic for processing as required by their operations. It is therefore important for systems thinkers to have a clear understanding of this logic and how it affects the systems operation and behaviuor.

Processes may be linear or non-linear being cyclical with feedback from each other. Processes may also be nested within larger processes or run parallel to each other.

If we are able to see the internal operations of the system, then we call it as a "white box" system. On the other hand, if we have no knowledge of internal operations, it is called a "black box" system. A black box is viewed only in terms of inputs and outputs.

Feedback Mechanism

Feedback mechanism is a fundamental requirement in all systems in order to regulate the output at a desired level. In feedback mechanism, the output information is fed back to the system to enable it to compare the level of output and then take corrective measures to maintain the output at the desired level as illustrated in Fig.7.5. Feedback is an important concept in systems thinking. Lack of appropriate feedback mechanism is a common cause of system failure.

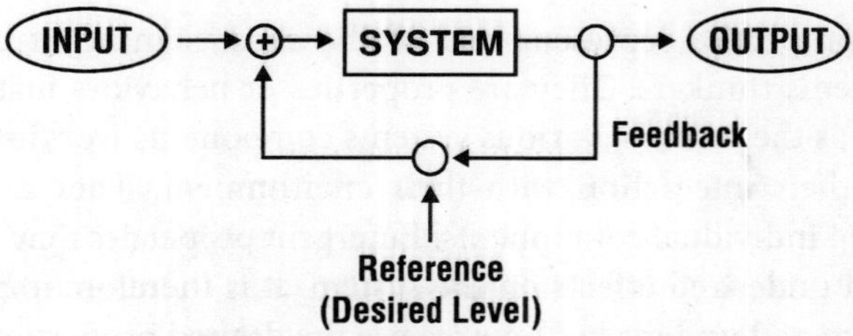

Fig.7.5: Feedback Mechanism

We can cite many examples of systems in our daily use that use feedback controls. They include water heaters, washing machines, air conditioners, cars, etc. Checking our bank balance to ensure that a specified amount is maintained is another form of feedback that guides our behavior.

Teachers use feedback of students to improve their teaching and supermarkets use customers feedback to better their services.

Another example of feedback control in business is maintaining a balance between the supply and the demand of a product. The more the supply of a product, the lower the price will become, which would be used as a feedback to induce the producer to lower the production. This feedback process prevents overpricing as well as over production.

These feedbacks are called negative feedbacks because they provide information enabling the system to act against any deviation from the desired level.

Homeostasis

Homeostasis is the ability of a system to keep an internal equilibrium in response to changes in environment. A system needs to have some kind of regulatory mechanism known as control system to maintain homeostasis.

This control mechanism will regulate both the internal conditions and external environments of the system and ensure that the internal processes of the system function at normal and equilibrium state.

Environments under which an organization functions are continuously changing and therefore the organization must have necessary mechanisms to monitor changes in the environment and be prepared with suitable strategies to face them.

Emergent Properties

Emergent properties represent one of the most significant challenges for the systems thinkers. They are properties or behaviors that manifest themselves as the result of various systems components working together as well as their interaction with their environment. They are not the properties of individual components. Emergent properties may have both desired and undesired effects on the system. It is therefore important to analyze them and understand how we use the desired properties and how we mitigate the undesired ones.

System Boundary

All systems have a boundary and operate within an environment. The environment, representing the sum total of other systems and input/output resources that system interacts with, lies outside the boundary of the system of interest. The boundary demarcates a limit to the system's internal components, their relations, and processes.

> *"94% of problems in business are systems driven and only 6% are people driven."*
>
> —W. EDWARDS DEMING

7.5 ICEBERG MODEL OF SYSTEMS THINKING

What is Iceberg Model?

The iceberg model is a concept that suggests that in many cases we cannot see or detect most of the details of a problem or situation. Only a very small amount of information (the 'tip') is available or known, while the bulk of 'real' information is either unavailable or hidden. This is how the expression "tip of the iceberg" is used in daily life. It means that we can see only small part of the whole situation.

The model gets its name from the fact that only a tip (about 1/10th) of an iceberg is visible outside, while the bulk (about 9/10th) of it is below the surface of water, i.e., invisible as illustrated in Fig.7.6.

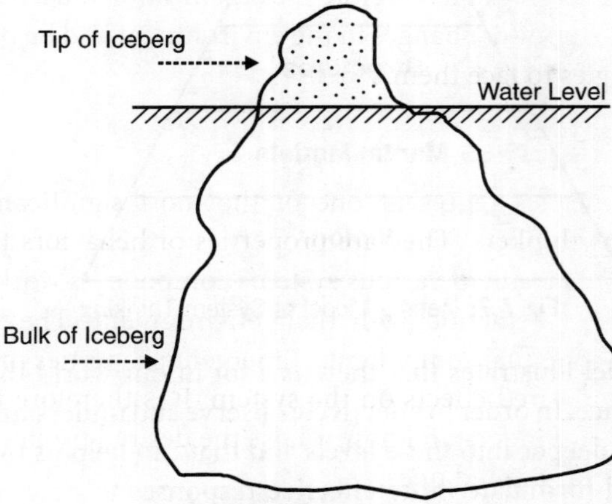

Fig.7.6: Floating Iceberg

[The British Titanic ship sank in the North Atlantic Ocean on 15th April, 1912, after striking an ***iceberg*** *during the maiden voyage from Southampton to New York City. The ship sank because the crew could not see the damage that came from below the waterline. It is estimated that more than 1,500 lost their lives.]*

Iceberg as a Thinking Model

The systems thinking process can be modeled or represented using the concept of iceberg with the following multiple levels of perspective as shown in Fig.7.7.

- **Events** – What just happened?
- **Patterns/Trends** – What patterns or trends are noticeable over time?
- **Structures** – What has influenced these patterns?
- **Mental Models** – What values and beliefs do people hold about the system?
- **Vision** – What is the desired future of our system?

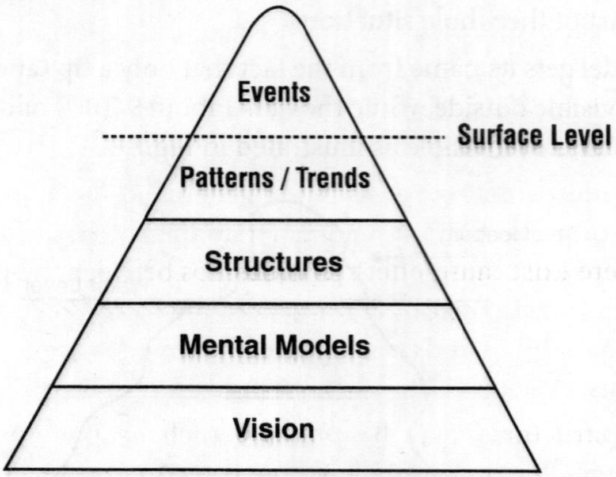

Fig.7.7: Iceberg Model of System Thinking

This model illustrates that there is a lot in our world that is hidden below the surface. In order to effectively observe and understand the world, we need to go deeper into these levels and that can help us make sense of our world and formulate more effective responses to new situations. In fact, this model can be looked at as a doorway to a new world of systems thinking.

Events

Events are the occurrences we encounter on a daily basis. Most of these events are routine, like buying milk and putting petrol in the car. But many other events may present themselves as problems, like a leaky waterline at our home, a fire breakout in our flat or a defective product in the assembly line in our company. Most of us spend our time at the event level.

When we view problems at the event level, our solutions tend to be *reactive.*

Patterns

A deeper level of examination reveals patterns of events or trends. Patterns are accumulated memories of events that occur over time. We can see the events as a series in order to see a pattern. We must look at the variables that are involved in the events and examine how they change over time. For example, we can see whether fire breaks out more frequently, or higher number of defective products occur in certain hours.

When we get to the pattern level, we can *anticipate*, plan , and take certain actions.

Structures

How do the patterns that we observe get generated? The structures that are composed of parts of the system generate the patterns that we see in the events. There exist cause-effect relationships between the parts. These are relationships where one thing influences the other. Relationships are harder to see than things and therefore we seldom go down to this level of thinking. At this level it is easier to *design* proactive solutions to problems.

Systemic structures may be physical such as the way parts are arranged or intangible such as the working rules and procedures.

Mental Models

Mental models are responsible for working of the structures. They are the assumptions, beliefs, and values we hold about the system. They provide the blueprints to the system to operate.

Everything that makes up mental models is difficult to identify. They might include attitudes, ethics, values, expectations, and experiences. It is therefore important to explore these elements in order to create a proper and effective structure.

The Mental Model level when properly understood and evaluated can help us create unique solutions that can *transform* the way the system functions.

Vision

Vision is our desired future of the system. It is the framework of thought that shapes and determines the mental models and provides a strategy to achieve our goals. Solutions generated at this level may be explosive in nature and may change and disrupt everything.

When we work through various levels of iceberg model, we may have to move back and forth between levels. As our understanding of a deeper level improves, we may get new insights and details about the levels above it.

The important message of the iceberg model of systems thinking is that every situation can be addressed at a variety of levels.

7.6 SYSTEMS THINKING WITH CAUSAL LOOP DIAGRAMS

Causal Loop Diagrams (CLDs) are used to conceptually model dynamic systems in a holistic manner by mapping causal relationships between pairs of elements (i.e., variables such as factors, issues and events) within the systems and showing how they influence each other. These diagrams would help us to have a holistic view of the system.

- Provides a detailed feedback structure ("big-picture")
- Identifies possible intervention points in the system
- Reveals the natural constraints within the system
- Enhances our ability to effect more realistic changes

Causal Link Diagrams

A basic causal link diagram between two elements is illustrated in Fig 7.8. A is known as 'cause' element and B is known as 'effect' element. The line with arrow represents the causal link between the two elements. When interpreting this model, we might say that when **A** increases **B** also increases. This is known as positive cause-effect relationship and denoted by "+" symbol.

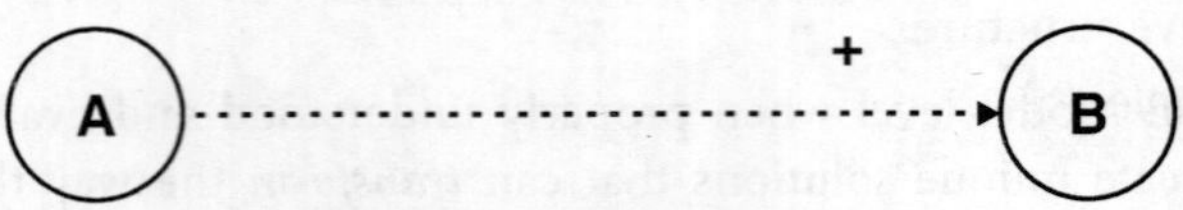

Fig.7.8: Causal Link Diagram
(Positive cause effect)

Examples:

Birth —+→ Population

Inequality —+→ Conflict

Similarly, we can also represent opposing or negative cause-effect relationship as illustrated in Fig.7.9. Note that the link is marked with "-" symbol. When interpreting this model, we might say that when **C** increases **D** decreases.

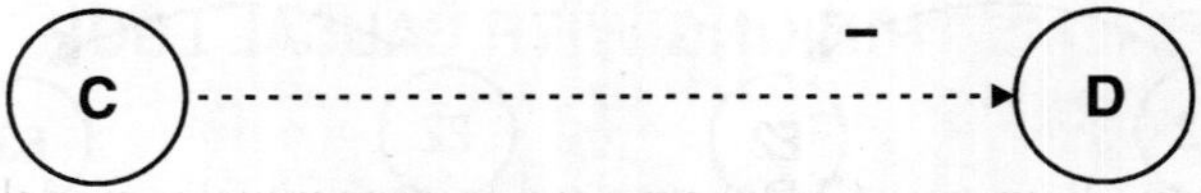

Fig.7.9: Causal Link Diagram
(Negative cause effect)

Examples:

Death $\xrightarrow{-}$ Population

Traffic Density $\xrightarrow{-}$ Population

Note that not all cause and effects happen immediately. Sometimes the effect may be delayed and Fig.7.10 illustrates the delay between the cause and the effect. The delay is denoted by a gap in the link. When interpreting this model, we might say that when **C** increases it will have a delayed decrease in **D**.

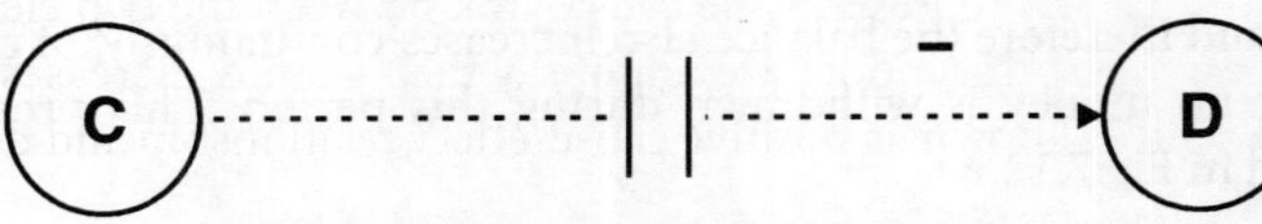

Fig.7.10: Delayed Causal Link Diagram

Examples:

Amount of Hunger —||→ Degree of Food Intake (–)

Population —||→ Death (+)

Causal Loop Diagrams

Causal loops are basically feedback loops that exist in systems. Since everything is interconnected, there are constant feedbacks and flows between elements of a system. There two kinds of feedback, namely positive feedback and negative feedback as depicted in Fig.7.11.

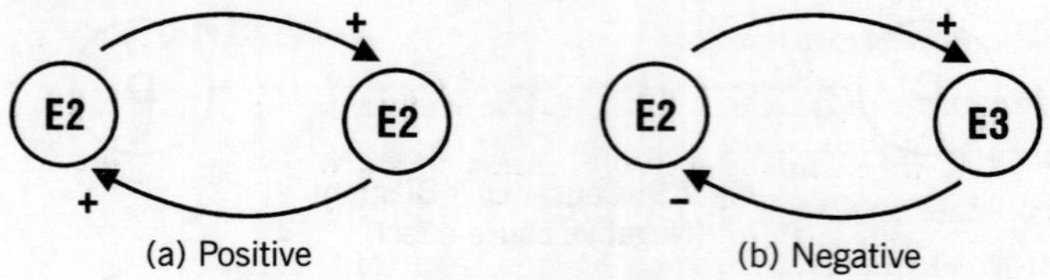

Fig.7.11: Causal Loop Diagrams

Reinforcing Loops

Positive feedback exists when the effect of the first element alters the second which then feeds back to the first to cause it to increase or decrease in the same direction. Such feedback loops are known as *reinforcing loops*. It means, successive changes add to the previous changes and keep the change moving in the same direction.

A typical example of this process is a Savings Account in a bank. If we have some balance money in the account, each time when interest is added the balance amount increases. This happens continuously over the time and therefore the balance also increases continuously, of course, assuming no money is withdrawn during this period. This process is illustrated in Fig.7.12.

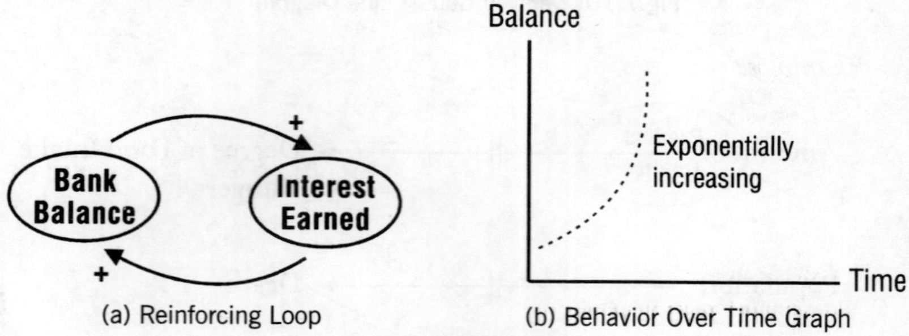

Fig.7.12: Reinforcing Loop

Balancing Loops

Negative feedback occurs when the second element sends a negative signal to the first element such that an increase in the second will cause a decrease in the first, and vice versa. Such feedback loops are known as *balancing loops*. It means, when the second element increases the first decreases due to negative link, which in turn causes decrease in the second element. This process will continue and the level of the second element will be stabilized around the predetermined.

An example of balancing loop is the maintenance of inventory level of a product by a factory. When inventory goes down below a specified level, an appropriate message is sent to the production centre to increase the production. Similarly, the inventory goes up, a message is sent to decrease the production. Fig.7.13 shows the balancing loop and the BOT graph.

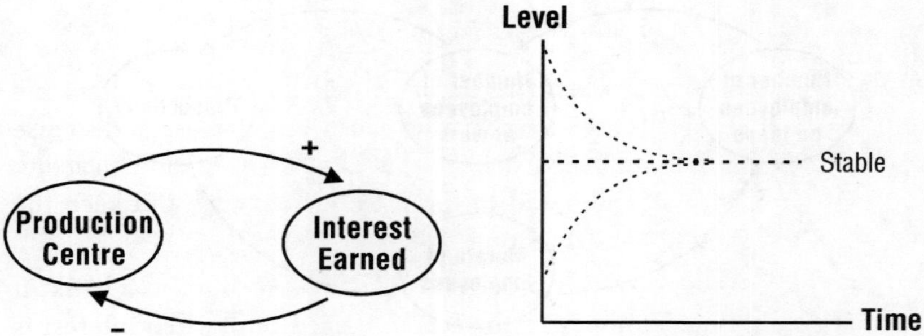

(a) Balancing Loop (b) BOT Graph

Fig.7.13: Balancing Loop

Another example of balancing loop is the maintenance of quality of a product and its customer demand as shown in Fig.7.14.

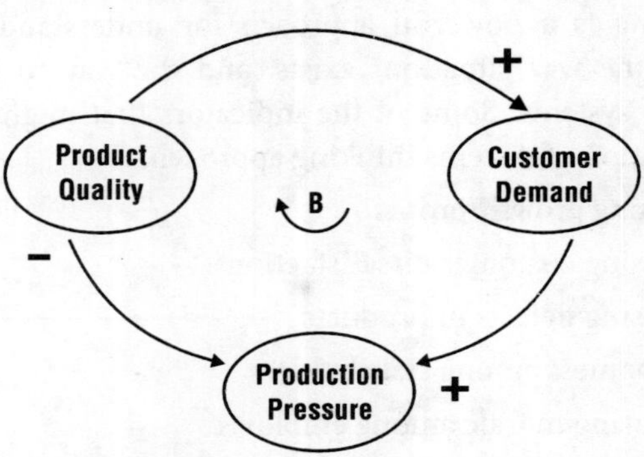

Fig.7.14: Maintenance of Quality

Some more examples are shown in Fig.7.15

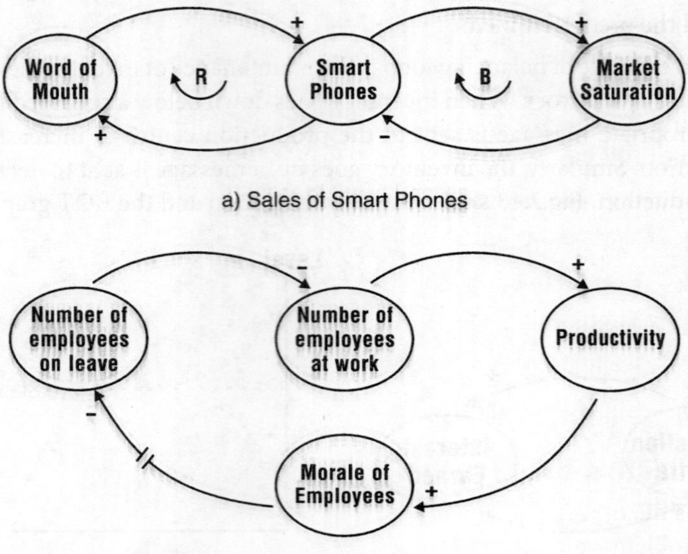

a) Sales of Smart Phones

b) Maintenance of Productivity

Fig.7.15: Examples of Causal Loops

7.7 A PHASED APPROACH TO SYSTEMS THINKING

Systems thinking is a powerful approach for understanding the way systems work, the way situations exists, and the way to improve any performance of systems. Some of the indicators that might suggest the need for application of systems thinking approach:

- Declining growth/profits
- Increasing customer dissatisfaction
- Increasing defects in products
- Unhappiness among stakeholders
- Decreasing morale among employees
- Threat of new entrants in the market
- Threat of new technologies
- Limited resources
- And many more

If we are interested in addressing a problem or a situation, we need to first understand the underlying structure of the system and then identify the key leverage points in order to effect any desired changes in the system. How do we implement the principles of systems thinking in solving a problem or addressing an issue? There are many different approaches of doing it. Suggested below is a Six-Phase approach to application of systems thinking.

1. Formulating the Problem
2. Understanding the Patterns
3. Comprehending the Structure
4. Modifying the Structure
5. Evaluating the New Structure
6. Implementing the New Structure

Formulating the Problem

This is the first step in any problem solving approach. We must first detail the problem we want to address. This phase includes the following steps:

1. Frame a detailed description of the situation and identify the scope and boundaries of the study.
2. Discuss with all stake holders to encourage openness and generate commitment.
3. Gather relevant information and data related to the problem from all the sources possible.
4. Identify assumptions and constraints, if any.

Understanding the Patterns

Next, it is important to understand the evolution of the problem situation. It is therefore necessary to know the patterns of behavior of elements over time.

1. Identify key elements.
2. Draw Behavior Over Time (BOT) graphs for these elements.
3. Develop causal loop diagrams to illustrate relationships among elements.

Comprehending the Structure

Before proceeding further, it is appropriate to develop an understanding of the behavior of the system. The underlying structure provides a view of the interactions between the elements of the system which are responsible for producing the patterns of behavior.

1. Develop a systems diagram showing the key elements and issues involved.
2. Document multiple perspectives on what structure is responsible for producing the patterns of behavior.
3. Identify key leverage points, where any small changes may effect a substantial change in the system.

Modifying the Structure

After a detailed analysis of patterns of behavior and a clear understanding of the relationships of various elements, we must now identify the changes required to address the problem at hand.

1. Identify the elements where changes are needed.
2. Most importantly, look for the leverage points where the least amount of changes will produce the greatest desired result.
3. We might also need to add a new link/loop that will produce desirable behavior or break an existing link/loop that produces undesirable behavior.

Once the necessary changes are identified, we must introduce these changes into the structure.

Evaluation

Once a modified structure is in place, we must simulate the new structure to determine whether the changes will produce the desired results. If necessary, we may have to relook at the changes and redesign the structure. We must also identify the key points that should be monitored over time to ensure that system produces desired results.

Implementation

The final phase is to develop a strategy for implementing the new structure. This is basically a change management task.

1. Prepare a report and present it to all the management team and stakeholders.
2. Assure those involved that the proposed changes are going to produce the desired results.

3. Identify additional resources needed.

The most difficult task is to change the thinking of the people involved in the system.

7.8 THINKING SKILLS FOR SYSTEMS THINKING

According to Peter Senge, the author of the famous book, "The Fifth Discipline: The Art and Practice of The Learning Organization", learning organizations must encourage holistic approach called systems thinking. As we have already discussed, it basically means the ability to see the big picture and to visualize the interrelationships between elements that might, at first, appear to be completely unrelated.

Systems thinking not only looks very attractive and interesting but also serves as a very useful tool for solving complex problems. However, as we have seen, it is not easy to apply it effectively. The main reason is that we need to employ too many different types of thinking skills at various stages of its implementation. According to Barry Richmond, the founder of High Performance Systems, Inc. USA, there are seven types of thinking skills that play critical roles in improving the quality of our thinking when we apply systems thinking approach to problem solving. They are:

1. Dynamic Thinking
2. System-as-Cause Thinking
3. Forest Thinking
4. Operational Thinking
5. Closed-Loop Thinking
6. Quantitative Thinking
7. Scientific Thinking

Each one of these thinking skills serves a different purpose and brings a different perspective to systems thinking approach.

Dynamic Thinking

Dynamic thinking is the ability to make quick and effective decisions in rapidly changing environments. Dynamic thinking makes a person to be curious always and to make intellectual inquiries all the time. This skill is essential to analyze the events and to understand the situations in terms of patterns of behavior over time.

System-as-Cause Thinking

System-as-Cause (or endogenous) thinking provides the ability to conceptualize the system as a whole and decide what elements are key and which relationships are critical in generating the behavior we are concerned about. This focuses more sharply on the internal working of the system and actions to be taken for plumbing the system itself.

Forest Thinking

Forest thinking is a way of seeing and thinking that acknowledges the presence of many elements operating together in a complex web of activities. It is a relationship pattern thinking and focuses on similarities rather than differences among various elements. In this way, we get to know the coherence, the relationships, and dependencies that may perhaps indicate a possible solution.

Operational Thinking

Operational thinking refers to a kind of thinking that focuses on how things work or operate. It is concerned about the nature of relationships between events and how patterns of behavior are generated. This kind of thinking enables us to identify key leverage points that could lead to a better solution. We need to concentrate on the "hows" instead of the "whats" and "whys". That is:

- Doing **things right** rather than doing the **right things**.
- Focusing on the **means** rather than the **ends**.

Closed-Loop Thinking

Closed-loop thinking tells us to see the system as an interconnected set of circular relationships, where something affects something else and is in turn affected by it. Closed-Loop thinking therefore leads us to consider causality as an ongoing process, rather than a one-time event.

Quantitative Thinking

Quantitative here does not mean 'measurable'. Quantitative thinking means assigning quantitative values to 'soft' variables such as motivational level of employees, commitment, etc., which are not measurable. Quantification can be done using a 5-point or 10-point scale. For example, if zero means very low motivation, then 10 may indicate very high motivation.

Quantitative thinking may help us understand the level of soft variables and take necessary initiatives to improve them.

Scientific Thinking

In study of systems, we often use models to represent situations or behavior of certain variables. In doing so, we make assumptions and approximations. Scientific thinking tells us that all models are only as good as the quality of the thinking that went into creating them. We must recognize that all models are working hypotheses that always have limited applicability and therefore must understand the limits and circumstances under which a model is useful.

7.9 PRACTICES OF A SYSTEM THINKER

Systems thinking is different from most other problem solving methods as it considers us as a part of the system we seek to understand and influence. Therefore, if we want to become systems thinkers we need to learn a new methodology and develop a particular way of looking at the world. The systems orientation would enhance our ability to apply the tools and methods effectively.

The Waters Centre for Systems Thinking in USA has suggested that systems thinkers must practice regularly a few system oriented activities that would not only encourage flexible thinking but also provide an insight into system behavior. They call these practices as 'habits' of a systems thinker. There are 14 practices that are briefly discussed here.

Practice 1: *Seeks to Understand the Big Picture*

Trying to understand systems as a whole, their purpose, inputs and outputs, boundaries and other environmental conditions.

Practice 2: *Identifies Connections Within and Between Systems*

Identifying key elements and their connections in systems would deepen our understanding of the parts as well as the whole system. And also understanding the connections between different systems would enlighten us with new ideas and thoughts.

Practice 3: *Changes Perspectives to Enhance Understanding*

Looking at the problems, experiences, and viewpoints through the eyes of others would broaden our viewpoint and understanding.

Practice 4: *Considers the Impact of Mental Models*

Understanding how our assumptions and thought processes about systems and their operations would affect the system results

Practice 5: *Observes the Changes in Patterns and Trends*

Paying close attention to the changes in patterns and trends help us understand the system operations better and thereby achieve better solutions.

Practice 6: *Tests Assumptions*

We all have beliefs and opinions and therefore it is important to test those beliefs and assumptions against others points of view. This would help us learn how to use listening strategies and testing tools.

Practice 7: *Recognizes that System's Structure Generates Patterns*

Taking an in-depth look at the system and its structure and understanding how patterns are generated would help us design new strategies to produce desired results.

Practice 8: *Identifies Closed Loops in the System*

Understanding the cause-and-effect relationships between elements and their feedback loops would enable us identify balancing and reinforcing behavior of the loops.

Practice 9: *Recognizes the Impact of Time Delay Loops*

Recognizing time delays in cause-effect loops is important to understand the impact of time that can have on our decisions and actions.

Practice 10: *Considers Unintended Consequences of Decisions*

It is important to consider carefully any unintended consequences of decisions and actions we made and decide their impact on desired results.

Practice 11: *Avoids Making Quick Conclusions*

Taking enough time to consider all the aspects thoroughly before arriving at a conclusion would help us achieve quality outcomes.

Practice 12: *Pays Attention to the Elements of Changing Behavior*

Behavior of some elements change over time. It is important to identify such elements and take necessary corrective measures.

Practice 13: *Identify Possible Leverage Points*

Identifying leverage points where any small change will produce large impact would help us create desired change with less effort.

Practice 14: *Changes Decision if Needed*

Understanding that there is always hope for improvement and willing to change decisions is very important to refine the results.

7.10 9 CS OF EFFECTIVE SYSTEMS THINKERS

A system may vary from a simple two-element one to a complex one composed of many different elements interacting with each other. As we have seen, complex systems have distinct properties such as nonlinearity, emergence, adaptation, feedback loops, and many more. In order to understand, appreciate and address the systems issues effectively, we need to possess certain unique characteristics that include the following 9 Cs, among others.

1.Creativity

Creativity is the act of generating new ideas and turning them into reality. It is the ability to perceive the systems in new ways, to find patterns, to make connections between seemingly unrelated phenomena, and to generate solutions.

2. Competence

Competence is the possession of sufficient knowledge and skills that enable someone to act in a wide variety of situations. It is the ability to comprehend and do things successfully to the satisfaction of all concerned.

3. Critical Thinking

Critical thinking is the ability to think clearly and rationally about what to do or what to believe. It includes the ability to engage in reflective and independent thinking and to provide an objective analysis and evaluation of an issue or a situation in order to arrive at an optimal conclusion or solution.

4. Collegiality

Collegiality is the willingness to recognize the concept of team work where responsibility and authority are shared equally by colleagues. The central elements of collegiality are respect, commitment, connectedness, and cooperation. It points us away from blame and towards responsibility.

5. Consideration

Consideration is the act of thinking about something carefully. It enables us to appreciate that systems problems often have multiple solutions and all decisions have consequences and thus guides us to arrive at a decision that is acceptable to all concerned.

6. Commitment

It is the quality of being dedicated to a cause, activity or purpose. It is basically an act of intellectual or emotional binding to a course of action. Addressing systems problems and arriving at optimal solutions warrants a full-fledged commitment on the part of systems thinkers at every stage.

7. Courage

Courage is ability to do something new that is risky or not popular among the people. It helps us overcome the fear of rejection and engage with the stakeholders effectively. It is often necessary to take strong stands in favour of solutions that are not popular or easy to implement but are effective in the long run.

8. Communication

Communication is the process of transmitting and sharing ideas, opinions, facts, decisions, etc. from one person to another or one organization to another. It is very important to communicate all our decisions effectively to the stakeholders in order to overcome any resistance to change.

9. Commonsense

Commonsense is the natural ability to make sound judgments and behave in a practical and sensible way, not necessarily based on specialized knowledge but based on simple perception of the situation or facts and the past experience. Many a times, systems thinkers might need to use their commonsense in understanding the events and patterns of behavior of systems and initiate appropriate actions.

> *"A common disease that afflicts management and administration the world over is the impression that 'Our problems are different'. They are different, to be sure, but the principles that will help to improve the quality of product and service are universal in nature."*

—W. EDWARDS DEMING

7.11 REVIEW QUESTIONS

1. What is 'systems thinking'? Why is it important?
2. What is a system? Give some examples.
3. What are the basic characteristics of a system?
4. Describe the IPO model of a system.
5. What is feedback mechanism? Why is it important in systems thinking?
6. What is iceberg model? How is it used for representing systems thinking?
7. What are causal link diagrams? Give two examples.
8. What are causal loop diagrams? Illustrate reinforcing and balancing loops with suitable examples.
9. Describe briefly the six-phase approach of systems thinking.
10. According to Barry Richmond, there are seven types of thinking skills that can improve the quality of systems thinking process. Explain them.
11. What are the habits a person should practice regularly to become a good systems thinker?
12. Enumerate the nine Cs of an effective systems thinker.

8 Comparison of Thinking Styles

8.1 INTRODUCTION

We use our brain, a most valuable tool, every day to understand things around us, analyze problems, make decisions, and navigate through the complex world. The brain uses the process of thinking when we try to make sense of experience, perceive and process information, make connections, ask questions, create new ideas or decide solutions. The type of thinking style that we apply during the process dictates the quality of our decision making, outcomes, and future. Our way of thinking decides how we perceive the world around us.

> *"The world as we created it is a process of our thinking. It cannot be changed without changing our thinking."*
>
> —ALBERT EINSTEIN

The brain is a complex, intricate organ which is made up of more than 100 million neurons and 100 trillion connections but weighs only about 1.35 kgs. It is divided into two hemispheres, left and right, as shown in Fig.8.1.

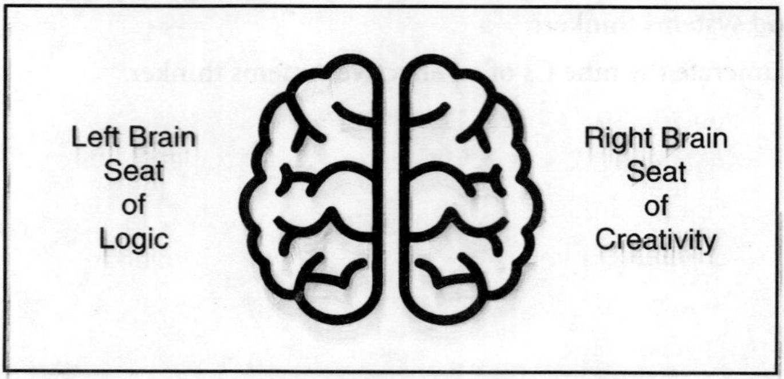

Fig.8.1: Structure of Brain

The left brain is considered to be the seat of logic and the right brain is considered to be the seat of creativity. Although the two sides differ in their functions, they communicate and collaborate with each other in a variety of tasks that the brain performs. The thinking style is a concept that describes the way the two sides of the brain perceive and process information.

The approach and process of thinking we use to solve a problem or implement a plan or strategy entirely depends up on the style of thinking we choose and employ.

8.2 TWO STYLES OF THINKING

While dealing with problems and issues, people predominantly use two thinking styles in their thinking process:

1. Logical thinking
2. Creative thinking

Studies have shown that the left side of the brain is more involved with the logical thinking process, while the right side is considered to be more involved in the domain of creative thinking. However, one side does not dominate over the other as it is commonly believed. Rather, they work together and complement each other to enable the mind to perform all functions. In fact, we do not use only one side of our brain at a time. Whether we are performing a logical or creative function, we would be receiving inputs from both sides of our brain.

Logical thinking is the process in which one uses reasoning consistently to come to a decision. To think logically means to move in steps from one related thought to another. Domain of logical thinking would include the following popular types of thinking:

1. Convergent thinking
2. Concrete thinking
3. Analytical thinking
4. Critical thinking
5. Vertical thinking

Creative thinking is the process of looking at problems or issues from a fresh perspective that uses the outside the box thinking to come up with ingenious solutions. Domain of creative thinking would include the following popular types of thinking:

1. Divergent thinking
2. Abstract thinking
3. Holistic thinking
4. Intuitive thinking
5. Lateral thinking

Logical thinking and creative thinking are opposite category of thinking styles. Similarly, types of thinking listed above can be grouped into five opposing categories as shown below:

1. Convergent Vs Divergent
2. Abstract Vs Concrete
3. Analytical Vs Holistic
4. Critical Vs Intuitive
5. Vertical Vs Lateral

Classification of thinking styles and thinking types are illustrated in Fig.8.2.

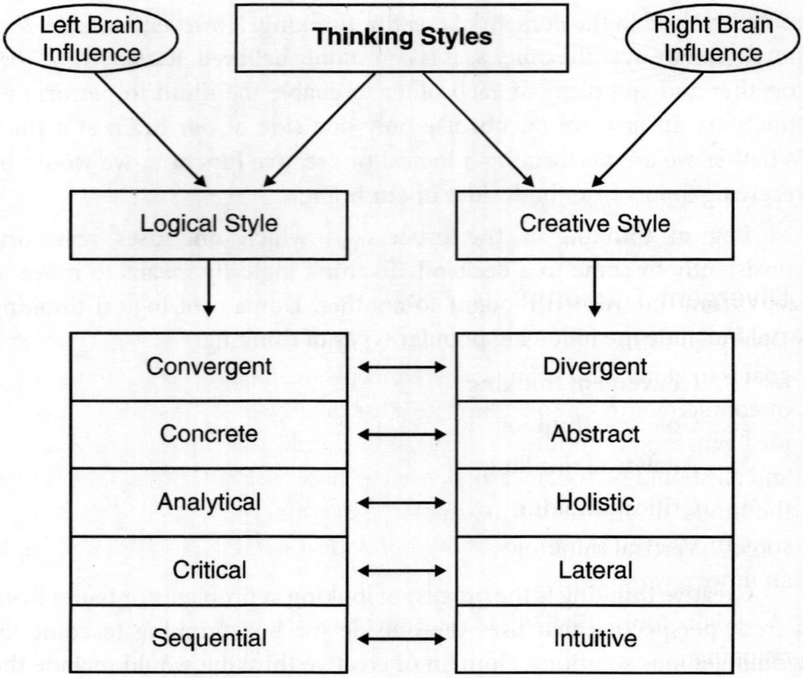

Fig.8.2: Categories of Thinking Styles

In the Figure, the double-headed arrow line indicates that each thinking type has an opposite but yet complementary counterpart. This means, when we try to solve a problem, we may have to use a combination of these thinking types together. In fact, in most of the real-life problems, we need to apply a combination of both logical and creative thinking powers to arrive at optimum solutions.

8.3 CONVERGENT VS DIVERGENT THINKING

Divergent thinking opens up imagination and creates all possible solutions, while convergent thinking analyzes and chooses the best from among those possible solutions using reasoning and logic as illustrated in Fig.8.3. In a way, they are the 'yin and yang' of solving a problem. Neither is superior to other.

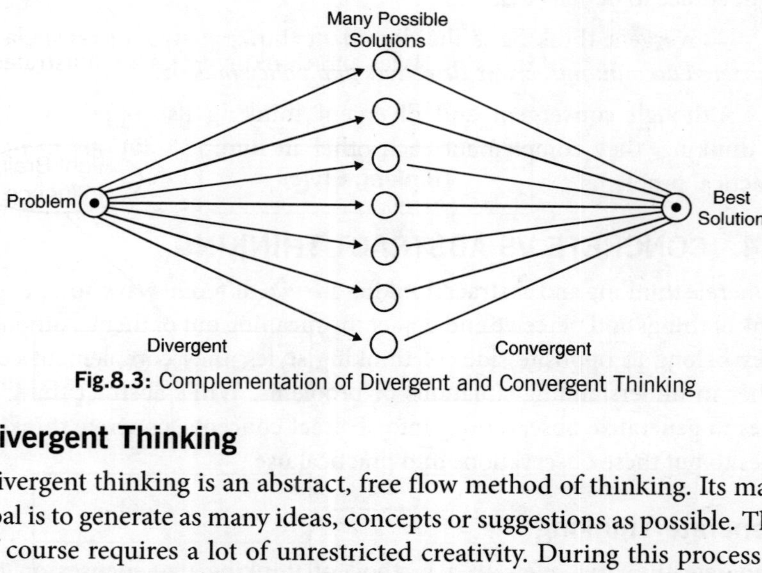

Fig.8.3: Complementation of Divergent and Convergent Thinking

Divergent Thinking

Divergent thinking is an abstract, free flow method of thinking. Its main goal is to generate as many ideas, concepts or suggestions as possible. This of course requires a lot of unrestricted creativity. During this process of idea generation, no idea or suggestion should be seen as wrong or crazy and all should be considered, no matter how fancy they may look. In fact, the motto of divergent thinking is "Everything is possible!". Remember, sometimes even a crazy idea could provide a starting point for developing an innovative solution.

Main tools used for idea generation are brainstorming and mind mapping.

Divergent thinking appears to be the dominant thinking style for *graphic designers, artists and writers.*

Convergent Thinking

Convergent thinking is a structured, well-defined method of thinking. The goal of this method is to combine a finite number of ideas or suggestions together in some organized, logical manner to find a single answer that is effective. It requires more of logic and reasoning ability and less of creativity. Convergent thinking may use known facts, previous knowledge and connections in the process of analyzing and judging. The motto here is "Choose is the best!".

A simple example of convergent thinking is answering a multiple-choice question in an examination where, out of many choices given, one right choice to be selected.

Convergent thinking is the dominant thinking style of *researchers, chartered accountants, crime detectives and policy makers.*

Although convergent and divergent thinking use opposing style of thinking, they complement each other in finding solutions to most practical problems.

8.4 CONCRETE VS ABSTRACT THINKING

Concrete thinking and abstract thinking are two different ways how people look at things and perceive and depict the meaning out of them. Although they belong to opposite sides of thinking styles, they complement each other in understanding situations or problems. While abstract thinking tries to generalize observations into abstract concepts, concrete thinking tries to put these observations into practical use.

Concrete Thinking

Concrete thinking refers to a method of thinking that focuses on the details of the items or things which represent reality as closely as possible. It is the ability to comprehend and apply factual knowledge. It considers situations or things as they are and involves thinking only on the surface, emphasizing literally on the practical aspects and to-the-point and very direct. To put it simply, concrete thinking is based on what the person sees as well as the facts. It does not go into the details of any hidden or intended meaning.

As an example, a concrete thinker, when looking at the famous Taj Mahal building, would say, "It is a beautiful building!". He will not be able to understand and appreciate the real concept behind the building.

This style of thinking is predominant among *practicing engineers, programmers, technicians and skilled workers.*

Abstract Thinking

Abstract thinking, unlike concrete thinking, goes beyond simple facts and surface details and tries to see the bigger picture of things or situations. It is the ability to look beyond what is obvious and imagine, conceptualize or generalize certain things. Abstract thinking is more creative in nature and involves a deeper, wider and multitude of thinking to bring out hidden concepts and make connections that others might find difficult to see.

Abstract thinking has many benefits as people who perceive abstract ideas are able to imagine things they do not physically see in front of them. Abstract thinking skills would help us to navigate our way through life.

Scientists, mathematicians, system analysts and architects use abstract thinking significantly in their work.

8.5 ANALYTICAL VS HOLISTIC THINKING

Analytical and holistic thinking use opposing styles of thought. While analytical thinking breaks whole into parts, holistic thinking sees the big picture as whole and tries to understand the interconnectedness of the parts.

Analytical Thinking

Analytical thinking is characterized by logical reasoning and involves mental process of decomposing a large problem or task into simple and manageable components. This enhances the ability to solve problems quickly and effectively using step-by-step approach to examine the parts and their relationships.

People with this type of thinking are great problem solvers and have systematic and logical way of approaching problems or issues.

Analytical thinking is the dominant style of *project managers, business analysts and programmers.*

Holistic Thinking

Holistic thinking refers to a big picture mentality and is characterized by perspective reasoning. It involves understanding of a situation or problem by visualizing its overall patterns and studying how they interact and work together to achieve the desired objective. Holistic thinkers tend to give broad attention to context, relationships, and external forces and situations.

When people develop business plans, entrepreneurial or innovative strategies, they think holistically and creatively.

This is one of the hardest thinking styles to apply and is developed by continuous practice and experience. The famous parable of 'an elephant and the blind men' is a classical example of holistic thinking.

Chief executives, managers, systems engineers, medical practitioners and political leaders use holistic thinking extensively in their work.

8.6 CRITICAL VS INTUITIVE THINKING

Critical and intuitive thinking use opposite styles of thinking. While critical thinking is guided by logical reasoning, intuitive thinking is purely guided by gut feeling.

Critical Thinking

Critical thinking is the ability to think clearly and rationally about what to do and what to believe. It is a process of skillfully conceptualizing, applying, analyzing, and evaluating the available data, information and ideas to arrive at the best possible solution. It means making reasoned judgments that are logical and well thought out.

Critical thinkers have the ability to engage in reflective and independent thinking and understand the logical connections between ideas.

This is style is predominantly used by *researchers, engineers and accountants.*

Intuitive Thinking

Intuition is seeing with soul. Intuitive thinking combines the power of heart, mind and gut to create positive thinking. This form of thinking is often referred to as the *gut feeling*. Instead of strictly following a series of steps, decision is made based on gut feeling.

This thinking style is suitable for making situationally relevant decisions when necessary data is missing for making an informed decision. Most often, such decisions turn out to be the right ones. Intuitive thinking is the fastest of all thinking styles and cannot be taught.

This style is suitable for those who are really involved in mastering a skill or craft, people like *designers, dancers and artists.*

8.7 VERTICAL VS LATERAL THINKING

Vertical and lateral thinking use altogether different, opposing kind of thinking approaches. While vertical thinking encourages a structured, sequential and logical approach, lateral thinking encourages an unstructured, imaginative and creative approach.

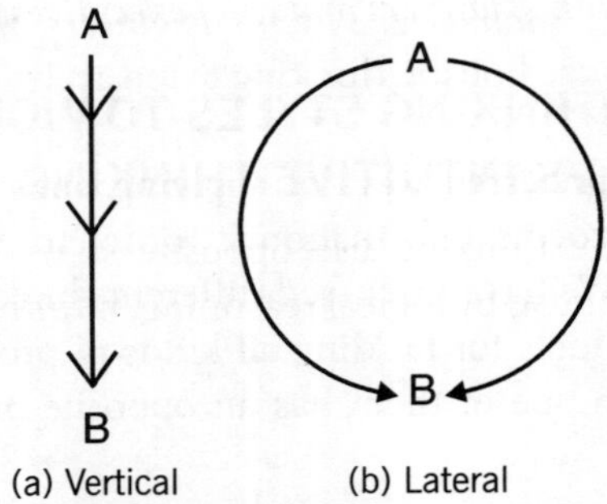

Fig.8.4: Vertical Vs Lateral Thinking

Vertical Thinking

Vertical thinking (also known as sequential or linear thinking) refers to the traditional process of thinking that applies specific rules step-by-step to solve a problem. It is linear and logical and uses only what is relevant and correct to achieve a goal.

Vertical thinking encourages the use of in-depth knowledge in a structured way and therefore this process of reasoning often serves well for scientific research and further advancement of scientific, mathematical and engineering disciplines. However, vertical thinking deprives of use of imagination and novelty which may lead to better solutions.

Vertical thinking is mostly used by *researchers, mathematicians, engineers and operations managers.*

Lateral Thinking

Lateral Thinking (also known as horizontal or nonlinear thinking) is the process of solving a problem by an indirect and creative approach. It involves generating ideas by looking at a problem or situation from a unique perspective and then arriving at a suitable solution. This form of thinking incorporates reasoning and imagination thus enabling the creation of innovative "outside the box" ideas.

Lateral thinking is not bound by logic. It breaks away from traditional modes of thinking and discards established norms and patterns. As opposed to vertical thinking, lateral thinking helps to identify different directions of solving a problem.

Lateral thinking is suitable for *social scientists, artists, film directors, entrepreneurs, consultants, lawyers and chief executives.*

8.8 PUTTING THINKING STYLES TO WORK

Thinking styles are preferred ways of applying one's intellectual ability and knowledge to process information in order to analyze a situation or solve a problem. We have discussed different thinking styles that can be used as powerful tools for tackling all kinds of problems, whether in life or business. Each one of them has an opposite but complementary counterpart.

Many complex problems cannot be solved by using only one style of thinking. We may have to use a combination of these styles together. We must therefore not only learn how to use these thinking methods but also understand where and how to combine them in order to achieve the best results. Remember, we cannot be only logical or only creative all the time. We need to mix them appropriately at times, depending upon the nature of problems.

In addition to solving complex problems, thinking styles are useful for individuals and groups in a number of ways. They could include:

- Generating novel ideas
- Designing effective systems
- Mobilizing people into action
- Building and strengthening relationships
- Achieving objectivity and insights
- Developing foresights

- Improving productivity and efficiency
- Cultivating people and their potential

The landscape of business and industry is changing rapidly and therefore we have to find new and better ways to connect, communicate, collaborate and work together. How can we make it happen? The best way to move forward is to cultivate the use of different thinking styles effectively. We must also try to understand the thinking differences in ourselves and others. If we do not acknowledge the thinking differences, communication and collaboration can be difficult. We should also be able to combine right-brain creativity with left-brain logic wherever necessary in order to arrive at appropriate solutions.

8.9 REVIEW QUESTIONS

1. How do the two sides of the human brain contribute to the process of thinking?
2. Enumerate the types of thinking that are classified as logical.
3. Enumerate the types of thinking that are classified as creative.
4. Compare and contrast the following thinking types:
    a. Analytical Vs Holistic
    b. Critical Vs Intuitive
    c. Vertical Vs Lateral
    d. Concrete Vs Abstract
5. Many complex problems cannot be solved using only one type of thinking. Why? Elaborate.